The two friends felt themselves picked up and
whizzed through the air. FRONTISPIECE.
See page 127.

WONDER TALES FROM TIBET

by
ELEANORE MYERS JEWETT

Illustrations by
MAURICE DAY

BOSTON
LITTLE BROWN & COMPANY
1922

PREFACE

The Siddhi-kur is a strange and mysterious creature! He is so old that we cannot even guess at his age, and he has traveled so many leagues from the land that originally produced him that we really do not know how much of him is as he was, and how much of him has been changed by time and place. Dusky little boys and girls in faraway India, long, long ago, were the first to listen to the stories that gathered around the figure of the Siddhi-kur, tales of wonder and magic which always ended with the hint of another, even better one to follow. Then from India, still in the unknown long ago, wandering tribes, or perhaps occasional single travelers, carried the stories into the highlands of Tibet. There they grew and flourished, till the Siddhi-kur in his mango tree, with his clever wit and quaint sense of humor, and the ever persevering Khan's Son, became as familiar to Kalmuck and Mongolian children as St. George and his dragon are to us. Some European travelers, hearing the tales from the people and realizing their unusual qualities, their picturesqueness, their fun and adventure, collected them and brought them home. They were first published in 1866 by a German scholar, Bernhardt Jülg, and it is from his pamphlet, "Kalmükische Märchen," and an English translation of the same ("Sagas from the Far East," by R. H. Busk, 1873), that I have drawn the following stories, changing and adapting them freely to suit Occidental ethics and taste.

I was first moved to put them into book form because of the interest they aroused in a certain small group of boys and girls to whom I told them, one hot, happy summer not so very long ago. The element of repetition, the distinctly human characters, the atmosphere of another land and

strange people, and the romance of quest
—these things give to the Wonder Tales
from Tibet the appeal to the childhood of
all times and all races, which is their
reason for having lived so long and traveled so far, and reason, too, for believing
they will hold the interest of our modern
American girls and boys.

ELEANORE MYERS JEWETT.

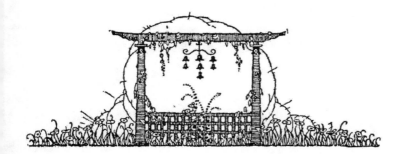

CONTENTS

ILLUSTRATIONS

WONDER TALES
FROM TIBET

THE CLEVER PRINCE AND THE STUPID
BROTHER

Long years ago there lived in the Far
East a Prince and his Brother, sons of the
Great Khan. The Prince was a wise and
clever youth, but his Brother was stupid
and ignorant beyond belief. The Khan
tried in vain to have this lazy fellow edu-
cated and finally, when all else had failed,
sent him to school to seven learned magicians who lived in a cave on the outskirts
of his realm. There was nothing in the way
of magic, either white or black, good or
evil, which these seven wise men did not
know, but because they had wicked, cruel
hearts, they left the good alone and prac-

tised their art only for selfish and evil purposes. They took the stupid Brother because the Khan bade them do so, and they promised to teach him all the art of magic, but inwardly they resolved that he should learn none of it and merely be their tool and helper. And so it was. For seven years the stupid Brother worked with the magicians, and in all that time he learned not one thing, so that at the end he knew no more than at the beginning. His brother, the Prince, thinking that all might not be well, went one day to the cave and stood all day long at the door, watching his Brother and the seven wise men at work. And so very quick and clever he was that at the end of the day he had mastered no small bit of the art of magic himself. Seeing, however, how things stood with his Brother, and that it was useless for him to remain longer, he bade him come away, and the two straightway set off together toward their home.

The mind of the Prince was full of the wonderful secrets of magic which he had just learned, and he was eager to try his power and skill at the game; so at length, as they neared the palace, — " Brother," said he, " go you to the old stable behind the hill, and there you will find a splendid steed as white as milk. I pray you, lead him gently to market, sell him, and bring the money to me, but remember this: *on no account* let him take you near the cave of the seven magicians! "

" Willingly," said the stupid Brother, and off he set for the stable. He was too slow and dull to be really surprised at seeing a fine white horse standing unhitched in an open stall where there had been no horses before; he only thought what a great pity it would be to sell the animal as the Prince had bidden him. Far better would he like to keep it for himself. At any rate, he would take a ride first and perhaps go to the cave and show his new possession to his friends, the wise men.

Scarcely had he formed this thought in his mind and leaped upon the steed's back, when the animal dashed off, swift as the wind, down the road which led to the cave of the wizards. Too late did the stupid Brother remember the Prince's warning to avoid that place of all others; he could not turn the horse to right or left, or slacken his speed until at length he stopped of his own accord right in front of the door of the cave. The lad got down and tried to turn the horse's head and lead him home; he coaxed and scolded and even beat and kicked the poor beast, but all to no avail. Then, looking up, he spied the seven magicians standing in a row and smiling at him.

" It is useless," said one, " you will never get that horse beyond our gate, so you might as well sell him to us."

" Very well," said the stupid Brother sulkily, giving a final kick. "How much will you give me for him? "

Now the magicians knew that this was

no ordinary horse, but in reality the Prince, who had changed himself thus in order to test his skill in magic.

By their charms and spells they had drawn him straight to their cave, for they were not at all pleased to find he had learned the secret of their magic, and now they were minded to destroy him if they could. So they bargained with the stupid Brother for the horse, paid him a good price and sent him away, never dreaming that he was in reality leaving the Prince behind him.

"Alas!" thought the poor Prince, "now is my last hour come! By all the hidden powers of magic, I wish that some living creature would come by into which I could transform myself and so escape!"

Before the cave of the magicians flowed a brook, and the Prince had no sooner formed this wish in his heart than a tiny fish came swimming by. Quick as a flash, the great white steed disappeared, for the Prince had changed himself into the little

minnow and was swimming rapidly away.
The magicians saw their prey disappearing and immediately transformed themselves into seven larger fish and gave chase.
In and out among the shallows and deep
pools they flashed, the little fish and the
seven great ones after it, on and on, and
ever the great fish gained upon the little
one, until the foremost of the seven could
almost seize it in his mouth.

"Alack-a-day!" sighed the Prince,
"now indeed is my last hour come! By
all the power of magic spells, I wish that
some living creature would come by into
which I could transform myself and so
escape!"

He had scarcely uttered this wish to
himself when a white bird flew low over
the brook, and in a flash the minnow was
gone, and the Prince was flying swiftly
over the fields in the form of a white dove.
But he was none too quick, for the seven
magicians had become seven great hawks
and were circling over him. The Prince

In and out among the shallows and deep pools they
flashed. *Page 6.*

sped on like the wind over hills and valleys, on and on until at length, quite out of breath and spent, he came to a tall shining mountain. In the heart of this mountain was a cave wherein dwelt a hermit, a wise and good man, whose name was Nagarguna. To this refuge the Prince now sped, and the hawks were almost upon him when he flew against the rough wooden door of the cave and beat his wings wildly upon it. Nagarguna opened it, the dove flew in and fell exhausted upon the floor.

"What is the matter, little creature?" said the hermit, picking up the white bird and holding him gently in his hands.

"I am pursued!" gasped the Prince, "my life is in great danger. I pray you, good master, hear me, and do what I bid you, that my life may be saved!" He paused to take a breath, and in that moment there came a knocking at the door of the cave which had swung to after the Prince had entered.

"Even now," continued the Prince,

" there stand seven men without, clothed in white. Before you open the door to them, let me change myself into the largest bead in that chaplet which you wear around your neck. When they come in, they will ask you for it. Give them the beads, but before you do so, break the string on which they are strung so that they will fall to the ground. If you do this, I can do the rest by my power of magic."

Meanwhile the knocking upon the door grew louder and louder, and so, hastily promising to do as the Prince had said, Nagarguna opened it. Without stood seven men with white hair and long white cotton robes. Very old and wise they looked, but their eyes were wicked.

" What would you, sirs? " said Nagarguna. They stepped into the cave and, looking sharply around, spied the chaplet of beads about the hermit's neck. The white dove, of course, had vanished by this time.

" I pray you," said the foremost of the

seven men, " let us have the chaplet that hangs about your neck. We have long heard the fame of you, have come from afar to see you, and would greatly like to carry away a token from you."

" Gladly will I give it to you," said the hermit, but in slipping the chaplet from his neck he managed to break the string, and the beads went clattering to the floor, all but the largest one, which still clung to the string. And all the little beads became worms and wriggled upon the ground, and the seven magicians changed themselves into seven large fowls and began pecking at the worms until they were all eaten up. Then, at length, the largest bead fell, and scarcely had it touched the earth before it became a youth, the Prince himself, who stood straight, tall and fair, with a staff in his hands. With this he slew the seven fowls quickly, one by one, and cast them out of the cave, where they became the dead bodies of the seven wicked magicians. Then he turned back, weary and exhausted, into the cave, but Nagarguna looked upon him coldly and with displeasure.

"You have done evil, my son," said he, "for you have taken life, even the lives of seven men; and it will not easily be forgiven you."

The Prince bowed his head humbly before Nagarguna. "Truly," said he, "I did not wish the death of these men, but they wickedly sought my life. Only to defend myself from a like fate did I lift my hand to slay another."

"Even so," replied Nagarguna, "and well I know your heart is not evil, and that only because you knew of no better way to defend yourself did you resort to barbarous killing. But by knowledge, my son, are all good things accomplished, all wrong ones avoided. Had your knowledge been perfect, you would not have found it necessary to take the life of any living creature, even in self-defense."

"Then, Father," said the Prince, "let

me stay with you and learn true wisdom.
I am sorry for this wrong, done in igno-
rance, and any task, no matter how hard,
which you want me to perform, I will do
faithfully to show my true repentance."

"Well said!" And Nagarguna smiled
upon the Prince. "If you keep this spirit
of humility within you, when the time has
come for you to rule this land, you will be
a wise and good king, and your people will
be happy and prosperous beneath your
sway. Come, now, I will tell you a task
worthy a brave man's strength and skill,
and when you shall have accomplished it,
you shall dwell with me and learn wisdom
until it is time for you to be king over your
people."

The Prince and the hermit forthwith
sat down side by side upon the rough floor
of the cave (for it was quite bare of furnishings) and Nagarguna told of the great
work which the Prince was to do.

"There is," said he, "in a very far
country a creature called the Siddhi-kur.

Very strange he is, being gold from his waist up, emerald from his waist down, with a head that looks like mother-of-pearl and a shining crown upon it. The Siddhi-kur is a creature of magic — good magic — and the land wherein he is shall be blessed with knowledge, wealth and long life. Now, if you can capture the Siddhi-kur and bring him to me, we will place him in a cool grove here upon this shining mountain, and then our people in the valley, your people and my people, will be mightily blessed above all others. They shall have gold in abundance, and what is far better, they shall have a great store of wisdom and knowledge, and long life in which to use it."

" That is indeed a noble task," said the Prince, " and with great joy will I undertake it. Only tell me how I may reach the Siddhi-kur and how he may be captured."

" Mark well my words," replied the hermit, " and I will tell you all."

For an hour or more they talked, and

Nagarguna told the Prince how he should go to find the Siddhi-kur, of all the dangers he would meet by the way and how he should overcome them.   And the Prince plied him with many questions and put away carefully in his mind all the directions and warnings that were given him. At length the master arose and, going into a dark recess of the cave, brought forth an axe, a sack, a cord and a basket.   These he spread out before the Prince.

" In this basket," said he, handing it to the lad, " are the magic barley corns which you will use as I have directed you, and also a cake which grows not less, no matter how much you eat of it.   The cake will keep you from hunger as the barley corns will keep you from fear."   Then, picking up the axe, the sack and the cord, he continued, " When at length you have found the Siddhi-kur, do not fail to tell him that this is the magic axe ' White Moon,' that this sack is the marvelous sack of many colors, in which, though it appears so small, there is space to stow away a hundred creatures, and that, finally, this is the cord of a hundred threads, each one different in hue, and each strong enough to bind and hold the mightiest ox. When you have shown him all these things, he will yield himself quietly to you. Arise then, my son, and start upon your way, and peace and good fortune attend you!"

The Prince arose, his heart high with courage, and slinging the sack, cord and axe over his shoulder, the basket on his arm, he turned to bid Nagarguna farewell.

"One thing more," said the hermit, "and this is more important than all else that I have told you. When once you have got the Siddhi-kur upon your back and are returning to me, remember, *open not your lips nor say one word for any cause whatever* until you have reached the door of my cave and have given the Siddhi-kur into my keeping!"

Promising to remember this above all

else, the Prince bade good-by to Nagarguna, receiving his blessing again, and set
forth with a quick step and a light heart
upon his great adventure.

Northward went the Prince, northward in a straight line as the crow flies, though the way was hard and rough, and many times he could find no shelter from storm and night. At length, when he had traveled a hundred miles, he came to a valley, deep and dark and mysterious. This, he knew, was the spot where Nagarguna had warned him he would meet with his first adventure. Gripping his sack, axe, cord and basket with a firm hand, he climbed down the rocky sides, though it grew ever darker and darker as he descended. The loose stones slipped from beneath his feet, and a great roaring sound filled his ears as he neared the bottom, where a muddy river rushed along. At last he reached the bank of this stream and stood there, wondering at the noise and rush of it and at the strange half-darkness that surrounded him. Suddenly the noise grew greater, and from the stream, the banks of the ravine, and seemingly from the air itself appeared great ghostly forms, very tall and fierce, and they rushed upon the Prince as though to kill him.

"These are the ghosts of giants who lived long ages ago," thought the lad, remembering Nagarguna's words. "I must not fear them!" And covering his eyes with his sleeve, he scattered a few grains of the magic barley corn in the air and waited, listening. The strange, ghostly sounds grew less, and even the roar and rush of the torrent seemed to become more distant. For some little time the Prince waited, with his sleeve across his eyes, and when the noise had grown quite faint and indistinct, he looked around him. No longer was he standing at the bottom of the dark valley with the muddy river rushing beside him! To his astonishment, he found himself, instead, on the top of a hill on the opposite side of it; the sunlight was bright and warm upon him, and an open meadow land sloped gently away before him. Casting one look down into the depths, at the muddy, horrible stream far below, he turned his back upon it with a sigh of relief.

" There is one adventure safely passed!" said he to himself, and trudged onward.

Again there was a long journey, and sometimes the way was rough and hard, and sometimes it was pleasant and easy. But northward still it lay in a straight line, and the Prince was weary enough when he had gone another hundred miles and had come to the second stage of his adventure.

He had reached a broad meadow full of tall lank grass, with a little stream winding through the center of it. On the bank of this quiet meadow brook he stood and gazed around, wondering, for the sunlight, so bright a moment ago, seemed to be fading. The soft babbling of the water grew suddenly loud and harsh, the air dark and murky, and there darted from the tall, rank grass on every side a throng of strange, ghostly figures. Very small they were and dim and vague, but their faces were ugly, and they swarmed around the Prince in countless numbers, as if they would cover and overwhelm him. He bent his head and gasped for breath, muttering to himself, " These must be they of whom Nagarguna told me, the ghosts of wicked dwarfs who lived and died long years ago! " He covered his eyes with his sleeve and cast the magic barley corn in the air, then waited, listening. The noise of the stream died down, and the sound of the rushing, ghostly forms ceased; and when the Prince looked about him again, he found himself on the other side of the little winding stream, with the sunlight pouring down upon him and the tall grass waving at his feet.

" There is my second adventure safely

passed!" thought he, and turning his back upon the meadow and brook, he journeyed on.

Northward he traveled still, and if the way had been hard before, it was ten times harder now. Over rugged crags the Prince scrambled, across bare deserts where there was no water and no rest for his burning feet, — only sand, sand, sand and a tiresome wind. On and on he went until at last another hundred miles had been left behind him, and he saw lying just ahead a beautiful garden. As the Prince entered it, he thought that never before had he seen anything half so lovely. Strange, brilliant flowers grew in rich profusion on all sides, filling the air with a soft, sweet fragrance. Birds with bright plumage flashed by, and the sound of their incessant sweet singing mingled with the splash of water in an unseen fountain. The Prince loitered along the path delighted, drinking in eagerly all the beauty of sight and sound and scent. At length, turning a corner, he came upon the fountain sparkling in the sun. Crystal clear it was and very beautiful, and beside it was a marble bench looking cool and restful. The Prince sank down upon it, for he felt suddenly very weary, but scarcely had he seated himself before the sunlight disappeared and a strange half darkness covered him. The sound of the splashing water grew louder, but it was very pleasant to hear, and mingled with it was a whispering and pattering as of small voices and tiny feet, and a brushing as of garments against the bushes. He looked around him and then stood up the better to see. From behind every flower and bush danced forth a little form, shimmery and indistinct but beautiful beyond belief.

" Oh, you lovely, lovely creatures! " exclaimed the Prince aloud. " But I must not look at you, for truly you must be they of whom the master told me, — the ghosts of little children who lived and died long years ago and were forgotten! "

Slowly and reluctantly the Prince, covering his eyes with his sleeve, cast the magic barley corns in the air and waited. The little silken sounds ceased, the splash of the water grew softer, and when he looked about him again he found himself standing on the other side of the fountain, with the garden behind him and a cool shady grove in front of him. And by a tree at the entrance to the grove, looking at him, stood the Siddhi-kur!

The Prince knew him at once by the shining gold and the emerald green of his body, by his head which looked like mother-of-pearl, and by the fair gold crown upon it. As he was looking at him, the Siddhi-kur turned and fled, and the Prince ran after him. Deep into the grove they sped, this way and that, and a long chase they had of it, until at last the Siddhi-kur reached the middle of the grove where stood his favorite mango tree, and before the Prince could touch him, he had

climbed up to the very top of it, and there
he sat, looking down and laughing.

The Prince waited only to catch his
breath, and then, seizing his axe, he raised
it high above his shoulder, exclaiming,
" Oh, Siddhi-kur, come down! Nagarguna, the hermit, has need of you! Come
down, I pray you, or with my magic axe,
' White Moon,' I will fell your mango
tree ! "

" Nay, do not so!" cried the Siddhi-kur,
gazing in terror at the uplifted axe. " Do
not cut down my mango tree with the terrible ' White Moon '; much rather would
I descend to you ! "

" Come, then, quickly! " said the Prince,
laying aside his axe and picking up the
sack and cord. On seeing these, the Siddhi-kur hastily climbed down from the
tree and stood beside the Prince, trembling.

" See, now," continued the lad, holding
the sack wide open. " Resistance is useless,
for here I have the magic sack of many

colors, in which, though it looks so small, is space to stow away a hundred creatures. You shall ride in it upon my back, and the neck of it shall be tied around your neck with this magic cord of a hundred threads, each of a different kind, and each strong enough to bind an ox. Be content, then, come with me, and you shall dwell happily in a cool grove on the shining mountain, beside the good Nagarguna."

The Siddhi-kur sighed deeply. "Resistance is indeed vain!" said he, "since you have the axe, the sack and the cord. So take me on your back and let us be about our way, for he who cannot mend his fortunes should make the best of them."

The Prince was overjoyed that his adventure should be thus accomplished so easily, and without more ado he settled the Siddhi-kur comfortably in the sack, tied the mouth of it with the cord of a hundred threads, balanced it upon his back, and picking up the axe, "White Moon," started on his homeward journey. Very proud he felt, and very well satisfied. He ate of the magic cake which grew not less, and being much refreshed, he walked bravely along, though the way was twice as hard as it had been before, owing to the heavy burden on his back.

After they had proceeded a long way in silence, the Siddhi-kur spoke:

" Of a truth," said he, " the way is long and I grow weary. I pray you, Prince, tell me now a tale, that the hours may seem the shorter to us both."

But the Prince, remembering how Nagarguna had bade him above all else not to open his lips on the homeward way, merely shook his head and said nothing.

" Oh," said the Siddhi-kur, " the Prince is wise beyond his years! He has learned the lesson of silence! Keep, then, your thoughts to yourself, but if you are minded to listen, I will tell you a story, a wonder tale, which will make the time pass quickly and pleasantly. Only nod your head, if you are willing, and I will begin."

Now the Prince was very weary, and the hours seemed long indeed. "Surely," he thought, "there can be no harm in merely listening, and perhaps the Siddhi-kur can tell a wonderful tale which it will be pleasant and profitable to hear." So he nodded assent, and the Siddhi-kur straightway began.

TALE ONE

THE WHITE BIRD'S WIFE

Many, many years ago, when the world was young, there lived in a country very fair and full of flowers an old man who had three daughters. They were simple, humble folk and owned little save a herd of goats, and these were dearer to the old man than anything else in the world, dearer even than his three fine daughters. Every day one of the girls went forth with the flock and tended them upon the hillside, and woe be to her if, when she returned at night, one of the little beasts was hurt or missing! The father stood by the gate of their yard and counted them all as they ran in at evening, and often he felt of each and caressed it, murmuring terms of endearment which might better have been spent on his daughters, to whom he never showed any affection at all.

One day, when it was the turn of the eldest to tend the flock, she returned at night, very late, and with eyes red and swollen with weeping. The cause of her grief soon appeared; one of the goats was missing, and the angry father lost no time in venting his wrath in shrill words of abuse and cruel blows. The poor girl crept away to bed, crying and complaining, but to all her sisters' questions she answered no word save to bid them crossly to be quiet. Yet there was something in her manner which led the other two to believe that she had met with some strange adventure, and they talked long together, wondering and guessing as to what it might have been.

The next morning the second daughter set forth to watch the goats, and returned late at night as the first had done, weary and crying bitterly, for another goat had been lost. And if the father had been angry and cruel before, he was twice as much so now. He beat the poor girl's shoulders with his heavy stick and cursed her till she fled in terror to her bed and lay there, trembling and weeping in the dark. But when the youngest daughter asked her gently what had happened, and how she had lost the goat, she was bidden to hold her peace, and could learn nothing. She noticed, however, that her two sisters now exchanged looks of understanding, and whispered much together, stopping at once when she came by. She was filled with curiosity and could scarcely sleep that night for eagerness to try her luck with the flock next day, and see if any strange adventure would befall her.

Early in the morning Ananda (for that was the youngest daughter's name) set forth with the goats to the hillside, resolved to be very alert and avoid all the trouble her sisters had fallen into. The weather was unusually warm and sultry, and about

noon a great sense of heaviness and sleep
came upon her, so that, in spite of all her
efforts, her eyes would no longer stay open.
She lay down under a tree, thinking she
would let herself sleep for just a few moments, but when she awoke she found, to
her dismay, that the moments had length-
ened into hours, the sun was nigh setting,
and while she had slept one of the goats had
gone astray.

"Alas!" she thought. "My father will
kill me if another goat is lost! I *must* find
it, though I hunt all night!" She began
looking hurriedly everywhere, in all the
pastures where the flock were wont to
stray, on the neighboring hillsides and in
the valleys, calling the goat by name and
watching in the soft ground for the mark
of his hoofs. At last, a long distance from
where the others had grazed, she found the
impression of the hoofs of a single goat
leading away along the muddy banks of a
stream. These she followed eagerly, hop-
ing with every step to see her missing

charge in the distance. The marks led
steadily on, and she followed farther and
farther until at length she found herself
in a strange country full of great rocks and
dark-mouthed caves. The hoof marks left
the bank of the stream at this point, led
directly to a cave in the side of a hill, and
there stopped short. The mouth of the
cave was closed by a big red door, and
Ananda, pushing against it, found that it
opened easily, leading into a passageway
dim and damp. At the end of this passage
was another door which shone in the dark,
making the way almost bright before it.
This, she found, was of solid gold and,
wondering much, she tried it and found
that it, too, opened readily. Beyond was
another passage, shorter than the first and
lighted by the radiance of the gold door
behind her. Ananda hastened to the end
of it, where she found, to her astonishment,
two doors, side by side, one of mother-of-
pearl and the other of emerald. By this
time she had quite forgotten the goat, so

filled was she with wonder and curiosity. She lost no time in pushing against the mother-of-pearl door, but, though she threw all her weight upon it, she could not make it yield an inch. So, turning with a sigh, she tried the emerald door, which opened at once; stepping across the threshold, she found herself in a large vaulted room, brilliantly lighted by lamps which swung from the ceiling. On every side were signs of luxury and wealth, soft divans, curious rich furnishings, and on the floor, in careless piles, gold coins and precious stones, — diamonds, rubies, emeralds and many others, beyond all power to count. Ananda rubbed her eyes, thinking she must still be sleeping. There appeared to be no living being in the room, so she began peering around in this corner and that, wondering more and more as she came upon one rich object after another. Suddenly she was startled by a voice quite close behind her.

She noticed a richly carved table in the corner with a
gold cage upon it.   *Page* 33.

" Good day, fair damsel! " it said. " May I ask what it is you are looking for? "

Ananda wheeled around in terror, but there was no person visible behind her. Only she noticed a richly carved table in the corner with a gold cage upon it, and in the cage a beautiful snow-white bird.

" Who could have been speaking? " said she to herself, still looking in every direction, and, as if in answer to her thought, the white bird moved on his golden perch and spoke again.

" Damsel, I bid you good day, and welcome to my dwelling. But pray tell me what it is you are seeking? "

Ananda stared in astonishment. " So it was *you* who spoke! " said she. " In truth, I hadn't noticed you before! " And then, bethinking her of the question twice asked, and not yet answered, she continued, " I beg your pardon — I have come to seek my father's goat which is lost. I followed his hoof marks to the door of this cave and had hoped to find him within."

"I can restore your goats to you," said the bird, "that which you lost to-day, and those which your sisters lost before you."

"Oh, you are most kind!" cried the girl. "Give them to me, I beg, and I will hasten home and trouble you no longer!"

"Not so fast! Not so fast!" replied the bird. "Wait and hear my conditions. Your sisters refused them with scorn and preferred to endure all the ill-treatment and abuse at home rather than to consider for a moment what I proposed."

"They must be hard conditions indeed," said Ananda, "to make me refuse them and go home goatless to my angry father! Tell me, good bird — what are they?"

"This is the bargain I propose," said the white bird slowly. "If you will marry me and live in luxury here, in my palace cave, I will send all the goats straightway back to your father. Moreover, you shall have all that your heart can desire, in so far as wealth can give it. Come, now! I will let you have fifteen minutes in which

to consider. Sit down upon that divan
yonder, and when your mind is made up,
speak and I will listen." Then the white
bird began busily pecking grains of food
from the cup in his cage, as if he had nothing further to say on the subject.

Slowly Ananda walked over to the divan
and sat down. "If I go home without the
goat," she reasoned with herself, "my
father will nigh kill me in his anger —
and yet, to marry a white bird, truly that
would be a very sorry adventure. But
(looking around the brightly lighted
room) life at home is poor and dull, and
here would be much to amuse and interest
me. And even a white bird might prove a
good companion, if I had no other." She
arose and walked back to the cage with a
decided step.

"I will marry you!" said she to the
white bird.

"Good!" said he, and rising on his
perch, fluttered his wings. Immediately
there appeared before Ananda a table

spread with a fine cloth and having upon it the best supper her eyes had ever looked on.

" Sit down and eat," continued the white bird, " for you must be hungry. The goats are even now on their way homeward and will find your father's pen unguided, with the rest of the flock, to-night."

So Ananda married the white bird and lived in the palace cave, and for a long time her days were full of wonder and delight. There seemed no end to the treasures around her, and she had but to form a wish in her mind to have it straightway granted. But after awhile she began to grow lonely. Every morning the white bird disappeared (whither, she never knew), and all day long she must remain by herself in the great vaulted room. In the evening the white bird would return, but after all, he was poor company compared with her two sisters, and she began to regret what she had done and long to be at home again. The white bird brought

her news of the outside world and tried to
cheer her by talk and gossip, and one time
he told her of a fair which was to be held
next day in a near-by village. Ananda
sighed deeply as he told of it.

" How I should love to go to that fair! "
said she. " It is so long since I have seen
any of my kind."

" My dear," said the white bird, " I think
it unwise for you to go; my heart tells me
that ill will come of it. Nevertheless, if
you greatly desire it, if nothing else will
make you happy, you shall have your wish.
Go to the fair and stay all day. Indeed,
if you go at all, you must promise me faithfully not to return until six o'clock in the
evening."

Ananda was delighted, readily gave
the desired promise and bustled eagerly
about, preparing for the morrow. The
next day she started forth bright and early
and in good time reached the fair grounds.
Such a merry time she had from the very
start! She made friends with everybody

around her, and having plenty of money to spend on herself and others, she soon found herself extremely popular. She saw all there was to be seen and did all there was to be done, and the morning was gone before she knew it.

Early in the afternoon there rode into the fair grounds a stranger on a snow-white horse. Very tall and strong he was, and good to look upon, and he was dressed in silk and cloth-of-gold, like a prince. Everybody began at once to ask everybody else who he was and whence he came, and it soon appeared that nobody at the fair had ever seen or heard of him before. All talked and marvelled at his handsome face, fine carriage and princely clothes, and wherever he went, a little crowd followed after him, watching curiously everything he did. Ananda saw him too, and when she looked into his face, all the happiness suddenly died within her, and she wished mightily that she had never come to the fair at all, for she knew that she loved him with all her heart. She wandered away from her gay young companions and stood watching the stranger from a distance and feeling very sorrowful.

"What ails you, my girl?" a thin, cracked voice suddenly said in her ear, and looking around she saw a little old woman, very bent and aged, and with a shrewd, wrinkled face. "What ails you?" she repeated, tapping the ground with her staff. And because Ananda did not seem to be able to do otherwise, she told her frankly the whole thing.

"Alas, good mother," she said, "I have fallen in love with yonder princely stranger!"

"And why should that make you unhappy?" said the old woman. "Why should you not hope to marry him as well as any other; you are a pretty wench, to be sure!"

"I am already married to the white bird," said Ananda, with a sigh.

"That is as it should be, my dear! That

is as it should be!" And the old woman broke into a cackling laugh.

"How can that be?" cried Ananda crossly, for she was quite bewildered.

"Because, my dear, yonder princely stranger is the white bird himself in his right and proper form."

Ananda could only gasp with amazement, and the crone continued, "He is bewitched, that is all!" And then she moved off as if she had done with the subject, but Ananda ran after her and, catching her by the sleeve, made her stop.

"Tell me! Tell me!" she cried. "Can I not break the spell? Is there no way in which I can keep him in his right form?"

"Let me go!" snapped the old woman. "Yes, of course there is a way! Go home at once, before he can reach there, and you will find his gold cage and perch and bird feathers in a corner of the vaulted room. Take these and burn them; then when he comes back, he will keep his man form forever."

Scarcely waiting to murmur her thanks, Ananda started for home, running all the way and arriving at the red door of the cave quite out of breath and exhausted. She soon found the gold cage and perch and the white bird feathers in a corner of the vaulted room, as the old woman had said, and these she quickly took outside and burned, until nothing remained but a little pile of ashes. Then she sat down happily beside the red door to await the return of the White Bird Prince.

Before long she caught sight of him riding towards her, and she jumped up and ran to meet him. But he, when he saw her, stopped short and looked down upon her very sorrowfully.

"Ananda," said he, "you have broken your word; you have come home before me. Alas, nothing but ill can come of it!" They moved on slowly until they came to the little pile of ashes which was all that was left of the golden cage and perch, and the white feathers. The White Bird Prince got down from his horse and stood looking at it for a long time in silence. Then he turned to Ananda and said, " You have burnt my bird form, my perch and my cage, have you not? "

" Yes," replied Ananda, beginning to cry, " but I did it that you might keep your man form forever, my dear husband."

" In burning my feathers," he continued, " you have burnt my soul, and now I shall be taken from you, and we can never see each other again."

" No! no! don't say that! " cried Ananda wildly. " If through my fault you have lost your soul, surely I can win it back for you! I cannot, cannot lose you now that I have got you in your own true form! "

The White Bird Prince looked upon her kindly, but there was little hope in his face as he spoke.

" Because you have burnt my soul, tonight there will come a throng of good and evil spirits who will fight for me, and at the end of seven days and seven nights the victorious ones will carry me away. And then I shall never be able to see my dear wife again. Nevertheless, there is one way in which you can save me, though I fear it is far too hard a task for any woman. If, for seven days and seven nights, while the good and evil spirits are fighting for me, you can beat with a staff upon the mother-of-pearl door outside our palace, without rest or pause for a single moment, then at the end of that time you will be able to break through the door and win back my soul for me. If you can do that, the good and evil spirits will be forced to flee, and you and I may dwell in peace together."

"Surely," cried Ananda joyfully, "that is not such a hard task, and for love of you, I can easily perform it! Give me a stout staff that I may be ready!"

That evening, when the sun had set, there came a great company of good and evil spirits as the prince had foretold, and they strove together outside the cave, and the din of their fighting was terrible to hear. But Ananda heeded them not. With a mighty staff she beat upon the mother-of-pearl door, all that night and the next day and the next, never pausing a moment, though she grew so weary she could scarcely stand or see. For seven days and seven nights she hammered on the door, and in the very last hour it began to give way beneath her blows. But in that hour her strength failed her, and she dropped exhausted and senseless to the ground and slept, unknowing, while the spirits carried away her beloved husband. When she came to herself again and found that he was gone, her grief knew no bounds.

" But weeping will do no good! " she said to herself at last. " I will rise up and search for my prince, though I have to go to the ends of the world to find him! "

So, drying her eyes, she took a stout staff in her hand and set forth at once, though she still ached with weariness and knew not which way to turn first.

It would be long to tell of her journey and of the adventures she met with by the way. Far and wide she traveled over the face of the earth, neither pausing nor resting, but ever seeking the White Bird Prince. At last, one day, when she was walking through a deep and lovely valley, to her unbounded joy she heard the prince's voice calling her from the top of a mountain. Quickly and happily she climbed to the top, though the way was rough and hard beyond anything she had yet experienced. But when she had reached the summit, her husband was nowhere to be seen, and she was about to give up in despair when she heard his voice again from the depths of the valley. So she hurried breathlessly down again, and there, seated beside a stream and waiting for her, was the White Bird Prince himself. With a cry of joy she ran toward him, and they kissed and caressed and were happy beyond measure, but their joy was short.

"My dear wife," said the Prince, "most grateful am I for this meeting, but now we must part again. The evil spirits have me in their power and have made me their water-bearer, and all day long I travel from the depths of the valley to the top of the mountain and back again, carrying water for them in a huge jug. And now I must return again to my labor."

"Let me stay with you!" cried Ananda eagerly. "Have I not gone to the ends of the earth to find you?"

"That may not be," replied the Prince; "nevertheless, since your love for me is so great, perhaps you can even yet win back my soul for me."

"How? Oh, tell me how!" said Ananda. "Nothing can be too hard for my love!"

"Go back, then," replied her husband, "go back to our palace cave and there build for me another golden cage and perch like those you burned. When they are finished, sit down before the cage and

sing, and put into your song all your love
for me. If your love is strong enough, it
will woo my soul back in the form of a
bird, and I shall return and take my soul
again, the magic spell under which I used
to live will be broken, and you and I can
dwell together in our true forms happily
and lovingly for the rest of our lives."

At this point in the story the Siddhi-kur
stopped short and said no more.

"Well, did she do it? Did Ananda sing
the song and woo back the soul of the
White Bird Prince?" asked the Khan's
son, forgetting in his interest all about
Nagarguna and his command to keep
silent.

"Of course she did!" replied the Siddhi-kur, "and her song was so full of love
and beauty that its like has never been
heard, even to this very day. But see now,
you have broken silence, my son, and so
I am free once more to go back to my
mango tree in the cool grove beside the

garden of ghost children. Farewell! And
be you wiser in future! "

And with that, the Siddhi-kur jumped
lightly from the sack on the Prince's back
and in a flash had vanished in the distance.

It profited nothing for the Prince to
rage at himself and his folly. There was
nothing left to do but to go back all the
way he had come and fetch the Siddhi-kur
again, for never would he dare to face
Nagarguna with his task unaccomplished.
So, taking a bite from his magic cake,
which grew not less, he turned about and
set forth once more to the northward.
Over the same rough road he traveled,
meeting the same adventures and passing
them safely by, until at last he came again
to the beautiful garden of ghost children
and found the Siddhi-kur sitting in his
mango tree and smiling down upon him.
Now, after he had captured the Siddhi-kur
as before and set him on his back, and after
they had gone far on the homeward way

in silence, that creature of magic spoke again, saying,

"Truly, O Khan's son, this is a long and wearisome journey. Tell me, I beg you, some tale of marvel that the way may seem shorter and pleasanter to us both." But, as his suggestion received no reply, he continued:

"Since you are minded to keep silence at any cost, at least you can have no objection to *my* telling *you* a story. I have a goodly one in my mind even now, and if you say nothing to prevent me, I shall begin at once." After waiting for a moment in silence, the Siddhi-kur began his second tale.

TALE TWO

THE PROMISE OF MASSANG

Long ago, there dwelt by the bank of a river a very poor man who had nothing in the world but a cow. " If only I had a calf too," he would say to himself, " I would be so much better off, for then I could sell the calf and with the money buy goods and trade with them, and in time might even become rich." So he wished and wished for a calf, and prayed to his gods and recited many magic forms; and every morning he went hopefully into the shed where his cow was kept, thinking he might find the longed-for calf beside her. At last, one morning he heard a strange noise in the shed and rushed out, feeling sure that his wishes and prayers were at length to be rewarded. What was

his surprise when he reached the shed to
see, standing by the cow, not a calf at all,
but a boy, tall and thin and very ragged,
with bushy hair and clear brown eyes. His
disappointment and anger rose at the
sight.

"What are you doing here, you young
beggar?" he shouted. "Trying to steal
my cow, I suppose — the only thing I have
in the world!" Seizing a great staff, he
went at the boy as if to kill him, and the
lad shrank back against the wall.

"Kill me not, master!" he cried. "I
had no thought of evil towards you. I am
alone and friendless and have come beg-
ging you to take me as your son."

The man put down his staff and laughed
loudly and disagreeably. "My son!"
said he; "as if I did not have enough to
do in keeping this poor body and soul together without taking upon me the care
of another! Son, indeed, when I wanted
a calf! Nay, I've a mind to kill you for

your folly!" And he advanced angrily toward the boy again.

"But I will not be a care to you," said the lad, drawing farther away. "I will bring you riches and happiness, far more than a calf could do!"

The man laughed again. "That is a likely tale!" said he. "Get away from here! When you show me that wealth and prosperity, then I'll adopt you and make you my son, but not before."

The boy crept to the door and there paused. "Master," said he, "you have grown bitter through poverty; but your heart is not so hard and scornful as are your words. My name is Massang, and I will come again and bring wealth with me. Such is my promise — farewell!"

The man went back to his hut, pondering deeply and in his heart regretting the harsh words he had spoken to the boy, while Massang fled away into the fields.

For a long distance the lad traveled, seeing no one and meeting with no adventures. At last, however, as he was passing through a fair green meadow, he came upon a man sitting under a tree, and the color of this man's clothing and of his face and hands was as green as the grass beneath his feet.

" What manner of man are you? " asked Massang, greatly wondering. The man put his head on one side and looked at him slyly out of small green eyes.

" I am a youth," he said, " of good understanding as this world goes, and I was born as green as the green meadows."

" Come with me," said Massang, " and let us live together, for I have need of you." So the Green Man arose and followed the boy without a word.

After awhile they came to a forest so deep and dark that they had great trouble in making their way through it. And in the very center of it they found a man sitting upon a log under a tree, and the clothing and skin of this man were as black as midnight.

"What manner of man are you?" said Massang to him. The man flashed his dark eyes upon him and said:

"I am a youth of good understanding as this world goes, and I was born as black as the black forests."

"Then come with us," said the boy, "and we will live together. I have work for you to do." So the three traveled silently on, through the woods and out again into the open country.

When they had gone a great distance, they reached a region of rocks and sand, very bare and white in the sunshine. As they were traversing this land, they came upon a huge rock, at the foot of which was seated a man clad in linen, very white, and the color of his face and hands was as white as the sand about him.

"What manner of man are you?" asked Massang. The man turned and looked at him, and his eyes were as pale and colorless as his face.

"I am a youth," said he, "of good understanding as this world goes, and I was born white — as white as the sand and crystal rocks about me."

"Then," said Massang, " we have need of you; come with us, and we four will live together."

Not far from this place the four companions spied a little hill whereon stood a hut, strong and in good condition, but apparently quite deserted. Here they took up their abode and lived quietly for many days without any adventures. Every day three would go out to hunt and one would stay at home and prepare the midday meal, each taking this task in turn.

Now one morning, Massang, the Black Man and the White Man set forth to hunt, leaving the Green Man behind them, and at midday they returned, tired and hungry. To their dismay they found the ground in front of the hut much cut up by horses' hoofs and the Green Man standing at the door, looking thoroughly puzzled and frightened.

" Alas! " he cried. " My comrades, we shall all have to go dinnerless to-day, for, while I was cooking the stew in the big pot over the fire, a band of horsemen came upon me and took all that we had in the house, even the pot itself. Come in and see for yourselves."

The three entered and, finding no sign of food, were forced to prepare for themselves a meal from the result of the morning's hunt, which was difficult enough with no pot to cook it in. There seemed no reason to doubt the Green Man's story, for the marks of the horses' hoofs were clear and plain in the soft ground before the door of the hut. But Massang examined these marks very carefully and then came back and spoke sternly to the Green Man:

" Comrade, you have dealt falsely with us. However it came about that you lost our dinner, I know not, but of this I am sure, no horsemen came to our door this day. You made those hoof marks yourself with a horseshoe. Tell us now the truth of the matter!" The Green Man gave Massang a sly, cunning look, but he said nothing.

The next day, having got another pot, Massang, the Green Man and the White Man set out to hunt, leaving the Black Man to watch the stew and get everything ready for the noon meal. When they returned, they found all as it had been the day before; dinner and everything to cook it in had vanished, the ground in front of the hut was cut up as with horses' hoofs, and the Black Man was standing at the door empty-handed.

"They came again," said he, "a band of many horsemen, and they took the pot of stew from the fire, and all else that I had prepared for you to eat. I was powerless to fight against them, they were so many."

But Massang doubted his word, and after he had looked closely at the marks before the door, he said:

"My friend, these are marks you have made yourself with a horseshoe. What adventure has befallen you? Why should you hide it from us? I pray you, tell us the truth."

The Black Man looked darkly and evilly upon Massang and answered never a word.

The third day the same thing happened. It was the White Man's turn this time to stay at home and prepare the dinner, but he had no better success than his companions, and had only the same story to tell them when they returned.

"I am glad," said Massang, when he had tried in vain to learn the truth from him, "that to-morrow it will be *my* turn to play at cook. Mayhap the same adventure will befall me, and then I shall learn why and how you three have deceived me." The three said nothing, but they looked at each other understandingly.

The next morning, having secured a new pot from a near-by village, Massang

Up the ladder and into the room climbed a little
old woman. *Page* 59.

sat down to prepare dinner while the others went forth to hunt. " There! " said he to himself as he set the pot of stew over the fire, " now may the adventure that befell my companions come also to me, and then I shall see whether or no I have more wit than they to meet it! "

For some time there was no sound within or without save the snapping of the fire, but scarcely had the stew begun to boil before Massang's sharp ears caught a little sound of rustling outside the window. He sat quite still, looking and listening. In a few moments there appeared over the edge of the window sill the top of a small ladder, and a thin, sharp voice exclaimed from without:

" Alack-a-day! Alack-a-day! What a steep climb! But methinks I smell a savory stew cooking within! " Up the ladder, over the window sill and into the room climbed a little old woman not more than two feet high, all shriveled and bent, and carrying on her back a bundle no bigger than an apple.

"Ah!" said she, looking from Massang to the stew and back to Massang again. "I pray you, son, give a poor old woman a taste of your stew — just a taste, and then I will be gone and trouble you no more."

Massang moved as if to give her what she asked, but catching sight of a very evil smile on her face, he paused.

"It may well be," thought he to himself," that this is a wicked witch, and if I give her a taste of my stew, she will carry off stew, pot and all, as she very likely did when each of my three companions was here before. I had best be careful." Then, turning to the old woman, he said, " Good mother, right gladly will I give you a taste of my stew, but it is now much too thick, and I dare not leave it lest it burn. I pray you fetch me a small pail of water, that I may make it the more savory, and then you shall have as much as you desire."

The old woman grunted, being ill

pleased, but she took the pail which Massang handed her and immediately disappeared out of the window.   But she left
her little bundle behind her.

Now Massang had purposely given her
a pail with a hole in it so that she would be
a long time trying to fill it, and as soon as
she had gone he went to her bundle and
opened it.   In it were a ball of catgut, an
iron hammer and a pair of iron scissors.
As he took these out they grew larger,
and by this he knew for a certainty
that she was a witch and determined to
deal very carefully with her.   He stowed
away the three treasures in his pocket and
put in their place a ball of ordinary cord,
a wooden hammer, and a pair of wooden
scissors.   As soon as he had placed these
in the bundle, they became as small as the
others had been.   Then he went back to
his place beside the stew and sat watching
it as if he had never moved.   Before long
the little witch woman flew in at the win-

dow, tossed down the useless, empty pail and stamped her foot in a terrible rage.

"Have a care!" she shouted, and her high cracked voice trembled with anger. "Have a care how you meddle with me! My body is small, but my power is great! Give me a taste of your stew at once, or it will be the worse for you!"

Massang looked at her quietly and did not move. "I am not afraid of your power," said he. "So long as you taste not my food, you are no stronger than I."

"Indeed!" said the old woman, stamping her foot again. "Do you think in your pride you can match your strength with mine? Well, so be it; let us see which has the greater power. I will put you to three tests, after which, if you do not cry aloud for mercy, you may put me to the same. Come now, do you agree, or does your courage already begin to fail you?"

"Not in the least!" said Massang, getting up. "Let us have the tests at once."

The witch picked up her bundle, opened

it and took out the ball of cord which she thought to be her magic catgut. " First I will bind you with this," said she, " and if you succeed in freeing yourself, you can do the same to me; if not " (and here she laughed scornfully), " you shall be bound to me, soul and body, to be my slave forever." Then she flew at Massang and tied his legs and arms securely with the cord; but as it was only ordinary cord, and Massang's strength was great, he very soon broke loose from it. The old woman howled with rage, but he quickly seized her and tied her fast with her own magic catgut, and though she struggled long and hard, she could not work herself free

" Enough! " cried she at length, panting and weary. " Loose me! You have won in this test, but it is only the first and the least; there are two more, and in these you will find yourself easily overcome." Massang unwound the catgut from her, and she sprang up, trembling and gnashing her teeth in anger, while Massang was

calm and quiet as if he were merely play-
ing a little game.

" Tell me, Mother Witch," said he, " are
you the one who has visited our hut for
three days past, and each time spirited
away our dinner and the pot to cook it
in?"

The little old woman broke into a cackling laugh. " Indeed, yes," said she, " and
your three fine companions had not wit
enough to save their dinner! One taste of
their food gave me power to carry away all
that they had, and I tell you, it was very
pity for their stupid heads which kept me
from bearing them away also, to be my
slaves and water carriers! A likely tale
they made up when they were ashamed to
own that a little old woman had got the
better of them! Band of horsemen! Ha!
Ha! And it was only little me! But come,
the second test, and if you fail in that,
young man, as you surely will, you will
die; there will be no mercy for you!" With
that, she snatched from her bundle the

wooden mallet, not stopping to notice that
it was not her own iron one. She flew sav-
agely at Massang and began to beat upon
his head with it, shouting:

"There, now! There, now! Cry for
mercy before I hammer out your brains!"
But the blows fell upon Massang's head
as lightly as the blows of a tiny stick, and
he laughed aloud, bidding her hammer
away, — it quite amused him!

At length, weary and breathless, she
paused. "And now," said Massang,
"you must let me do the same to you!"
Taking the witch's iron hammer from his
pocket, he brought it down upon her head
with great force.

The old woman clapped her hands to
her head, uttered a shriek, leaped into the
air and flew out through the window. Just
at that minute the Black Man, the Green
Man and the White Man, having returned
from the hunt, appeared in the doorway.

"Quick! Quick!" cried Massang,
pushing past them. "Let us follow the

little witch woman! She is wounded and will fly right to her lair. Come with me, quick, and follow her!" So the four dashed out of the hut and after the old witch as fast as they could go. She flew low in the sky like a great bird, and every now and then a drop of black blood fell to the ground from the wound in her head. At first she flew so fast that Massang, with the other three behind him, had great difficulty in keeping up with her, but after awhile she began to waver and fly unevenly. By this time the four found themselves running over a barren stretch of land, very rough and uneven, and they stumbled and fell more than once, but as the flight of the witch became ever slower, they managed to keep her in sight. At last they saw her fall to the ground and lie quite still, and running up to her, they found she was dead.

"An evil old witch," said Massang, "yet I meant not to kill her — only to wound and drive her away."

" She would have killed you quickly
enough," said the three, " and us too, if
we had let her! "

Looking around them, they saw near
by the mouth of a deep, dark cave.

" This must be her lair," said Massang,
" and no doubt it is filled with treasure;
let us go down and see." But apparently
there was no way of getting down. The
cave was so deep they could scarcely see
the bottom of it, and the sides were steep
and smooth as polished marble.

Massang, however, found that he still
had in his pocket the ball of magic catgut.
This he unwound and, finding it would
reach to the bottom of the cave, bade his
companions hold one end of it firmly while
he climbed down upon it. Inside the cave
the light was very dim, but as soon as his
eyes became accustomed to it, he saw, lying
in great heaps upon the floor, gold and
silver, diamonds, rubies, emeralds and all
manner of precious stones. He shouted
joyfully up to his companions, who were

leaning over the mouth of the cave. " Fetch bags," said he, " big bags, and I will fill them with treasure; then you shall pull them up with the catgut, and afterwards we will divide the spoil and be all four rich and prosperous for the rest of our lives! "

The three men hurried back to the hut to get bags, and while they were gone, Massang roamed around the cave, which was large and full of dark corners heaped high with treasure. He had scarcely finished looking about when he heard the Green Man shouting to him from above. Then bags were thrown down, and he filled them to the brim with gleaming gold and precious stones. All the rest of the day until darkness covered them, they were busy, Massang filling bags and the three men hauling them up, emptying them and sending them down again to be refilled. At last Massang called up, saying it was too dark for him to see further, and the cave was pretty well cleared out, anyway. He fastened the catgut around his waist and bade his companions draw him up. But to his dismay he saw the Green Man leaning over the mouth of the cave, with an evil smile on his face and a knife in his hand.

"Now, Master Massang," said the Green Man, and his voice sounded harsh and cruel, "if you think we are going to drag you up to share the spoil, you are much mistaken! There will be just so much more for us if you are not here! So farewell, and peace be to your bones. You will never be able to get out of this cave to tell tales on us!"

With that he cut the catgut and disappeared, and Massang could hear the three talking together and then moving away. All night long he could hear them coming and going. Evidently they were bearing away the treasure. When morning came, there was not a sound, and Massang knew that he was quite deserted. He sat down on the floor of the cave and buried his face in his hands, and his heart was very heavy.

But after a while he got up and looked around, thinking that he would not despair until he had made sure there was no possible way of getting out of the cave. A careful search showed him there was nothing left to make use of but a handful of neglected gold and three cherry pits. These he picked up. " It is my last and only hope," he thought, and aloud he said, " By all the power of good magic, I wish that I may find a way out of this cave to light and freedom." Then he buried the cherry pits directly beneath the mouth of the cave. Scarcely had he done so when a great wave of drowsiness came over him and, lying down on the ground, in a few moments he fell into a deep, dreamless sleep.

When he awoke he found to his astonishment three young cherry trees standing tall and straight beside him, and the top of the tallest of these reached up to the mouth of the cave. He jumped up joyfully and stretched himself. In reality he had been asleep for several years, yet it seemed no more to him than so many hours. It was easy enough now to climb up the cherry tree and out of the cave, and glad indeed he was to be free again and out in the sunshine. He tramped eagerly along until he came to a hut where he bought food, paying for it with some of the gold which he had brought up in his pockets from the witch's cave.

It were long to tell of all Massang's wanderings after that. He traveled far and wide, ever searching for his false companions, until at last, after many weeks, he came upon three very elegant houses surrounded by beautiful grounds, and with every sign of prosperity and wealth about them. These houses, he soon learned, belonged to his wicked friends, — the Green Man, the Black Man and the White Man. At the time all three were away upon a hunting trip, so Massang procured a stout staff and took up his stand by a gateway through which they must pass on their way home.

He had not waited very long before he spied them in the distance, coming toward him. They walked gaily enough, never thinking of trouble, and did not even see him until they had got quite close to him. Massang stood directly in their path, his staff in his hands. The Green Man saw him first and, giving a cry of fear, fell at his feet. Then the other two saw him, and they also fell trembling before him. " It is Massang," they cried, " or his ghost come for vengeance! Surely now we are doomed! "

" Get up! " said Massang sternly, touching them with his staff. " Get up! I am no ghost but Massang indeed, whom you left to die miserably in the witch's cave. I had intended to slay you with this staff, for your falseness and cruelty — but you are too base and cowardly to touch! "

The three still lay trembling and grovelling upon the ground. " Alas! good

Master," cried the Black Man, " we have suffered enough already because of our evil deed. With all our wealth we have been wretchedly unhappy and have found neither peace by day nor sleep by night! "

" That is indeed true! " groaned the White Man. " We will give you all our wealth and become beggars, if you will but forgive us and let us go away unharmed." And even the Green Man nodded his head in token of agreement. At this the heart of Massang was softened.

" Come! " said he. " Get up and we will talk it over." And when they had risen to their feet, he said, " This much I will require of you; let each of you take half of his wealth and go with it to the bank of a certain river. There you will find a poor man who has nothing in all the world save only one cow. Give him the treasure that you have brought, and say to him, ' Your son, Massang, sends you wealth and prosperity with his love.' Do this faithfully, and I will freely forgive you."

The men readily promised to do all that Massang had bidden them, and in a few days he saw for himself the three starting forth at the head of a great train of mules laden with wealth and treasure of every sort.

" And did they find the poor man with the one cow?" asked the Khan's son. " Go on! You haven't finished!"

" Yes, they found him," said the Siddhi-kur, with a laugh. " And they poured out their wealth before him, and when Massang came shortly afterwards, you may be sure the old man received him and kept him as a well loved son.

" But you, O Prince, you have forgotten the words of the wise Nagarguna! You have broken silence on the homeward way, and so now you have no further power over me." With a shout of joy, the Siddhi-kur leaped from the bag on the

Prince's back and sped away into the distance. Nor did the Khan's son set eyes on him again until he had retraced his steps through all the dangers and hardships he had met before and stood once more under the mango tree in the cool grove beside the garden of ghost children.

Seeing him so persistent in his mission, the Siddhi-kur made no objections to being taken again, and allowed himself to be tied into the magic bag with the cord of a hundred threads and tossed once more on to the Prince's back. After they had traveled a long time in silence and were both grown weary, he suggested again that some wonder tale be told, and receiving no answer from the Prince but a nod of agreement, he began at once.

TALE THREE

In a far country, many years ago, there lived six young men who were fast friends. One was a Magician's son, one a Blacksmith's son, the third a Doctor's son, the fourth the son of a Woodcarver, the fifth the son of a Painter, and the sixth the son of a Prince. Now all these six lads intended to follow the lives and the work of their fathers, but before settling down, they all desired to seek some great adventure.

"Let us go forth together," said they, "and travel into some strange country, and then perhaps something wonderful may befall us which will make us rich to the end of our days, or at least give us a goodly tale to tell our neighbors when we shall have returned and taken up our fathers' work."

So it was agreed among them, and on a certain day, very early in the morning, all six started out together. For several days they traveled, choosing always the least known road and going farther and farther from the country they knew into the unfamiliar lands beyond. Yet no adventure whatever befell them.

At last they came to a small, round pond into which six streams emptied, each coming from a different direction. Then said the Blacksmith's son:

"Friends, here are six rivers, one for each of us. Suppose we separate, each choosing one stream and following it alone to its source. It may be that Dame Adventure is shy and will not meet us all together, whereas to each of us apart she will bring some rare happening."

This saying pleased the other five, and they agreed at once. "Moreover," said the Magician's son, "let us each plant a small tree at the mouth of his chosen river, and I will weave a spell upon them all so that if aught evil befalls its planter, that tree will wither away."

"Splendid!" said the Doctor's son, "and let us agree to return to this spot at the end of a year and a day. And when we are met, if any one of us is absent and his tree withered, we will straightway follow his stream and try to rescue him from his danger."

The other friends were greatly pleased at these suggestions, and each of the six set about at once choosing a tree and planting it at the mouth of one of the streams. When the trees were all planted, the young men took their stand beside their respective streams while the Magician's son went around from one tree to another, weaving a magic spell about it so that it would wither and die if any ill came to the one who had planted it. Then, with many handshakes and words of faithfulness and affection, the six friends parted, each one disappearing up the bank of the river he had selected.

Now we shall follow the fortunes of the Prince's son. The underbrush along the bank of his stream was thick and heavy, so that he must needs walk slowly and with difficulty. All day long he wandered on, finding no open space, and hearing nothing but the sound of the water babbling beside him. At length, however, the banks of the little river began to widen out, and toward sunset he found himself in an open meadow, with an old broken well in the middle of it and a dark forest beyond. He was tired and warm with the long hard walk through the underbrush, so when he had reached the well, he sat down beside it to rest and cool himself. He had not been there long before he saw approaching him a tall and exceedingly beautiful girl with a water pitcher on her shoulder. Her hair was very long and black, she was clothed in flowing white linen gar-

ments, and she moved across the field bare-
footed, with a light, lithe step. And marvellous to behold, wherever her foot
pressed the soft earth, a white flower
sprang into bloom, marking her course
across the meadow in a trail of beauty.
While the Prince's son was wondering at
this and at the unusual loveliness of the
girl, she drew up to the well and lowered
her pitcher from her shoulder. He jumped
up at once and, taking it from her hand,
offered to draw the water for her. She
said not a word, but when the pitcher was
full, she set forth again across the meadow,
leaving him to follow her and carry it.
Over the field and into the woods they
went, in the deepening twilight. The
maiden moved with a sure step, quickly
and easily among the trees, but the Prince's
son had great trouble in following her,
often stumbling in the darkness and finding the pitcher of water ever heavier and
harder to carry. At last it grew so dark
in the woods that he could see nothing at

Quite unexpectedly they came at length to a little
log hut. *Page* 81.

all except the gleam of the girl's white dress before him, and the water pitcher became so heavy that his shoulder well-nigh broke with the weight of it, but he struggled on, determined not to lose sight of his strange and beautiful guide.

Quite unexpectedly they came at length to a little log hut with a candle shining in the window. As they approached it, the door was opened by an old man, white-haired, shriveled and bent, with an old, wrinkled woman beside him.

" Come in, daughter," said the aged man, motioning to the girl. " Have you brought the Prince's son? "

" That I have, Father," she replied, and her voice was as lovely as her beautiful face. The Prince's son entered the little hut, wondering greatly, and the door was closed behind him.

Without a word of explanation, the aged couple made haste to set before him a simple, hearty supper, the girl having disappeared meanwhile into an inner room.

When he had finished, as if in answer to his unspoken thought, the old man said:

"You are doubtless wondering, my son, about the lovely damsel who abides here with us, and whom you have followed this day to our humble door. But in truth, sir, it is little enough we can tell your ourselves. Whence she comes, we know not, though we have cherished and reared her as our own child. Several years ago we found her on our doorstep, a little laughing maid as fair-as ever the sun looked on, and clothed in the softest, richest raiment. Right joyfully we took her in, and she dwelt with us happily day by day, yet never did she say a word by which we might know whose child she was. A king's daughter she must be, or the child of some good spirit. Of late she has spoken much of a change to come in her life, of a Prince's son, and of many other things which we have not understood, but our hearts have been sad within us, fearing lest the girl prophesied her marriage and separation from us who love her more than all else in the whole world."

At this point the Prince's son eagerly interrupted the old man, saying, " I pray you, Father, be no longer sad, but hear the great desire of my heart. I am indeed the son of a Prince, and the maiden is in my eyes the loveliest and most beautiful creature in the universe. Having once seen her, I have no further wish in life than to marry her and live peacefully with her here in this forest, in a house that I shall build for her with my own hands, near by this hut. Surely the fates have decreed that this shall be, for have I not traveled far this day in search of whatsoever Dame Fortune might have in store for me?"

" So be it," said the other; " needs must you be the destined bridegroom, the son of a Prince, for had it been otherwise our daughter never would have led you through the dark forest to our lonely home. Let the blessing of an old man rest upon you."

And so it came about that the Prince's son married the beautiful maiden of the woods and lived with her in peace and happiness in a little log house hard by her foster-father's hut. Days passed by, and weeks, and ever the two grew more loving and contented, and it seemed as if nothing could mar the even joy of their lives. But, alas, one day a great misfortune befell them!

It was warm and sultry, and the two had strolled hand in hand down to the bank of a rushing stream that ran through the forest. Now the water looked so very cool and refreshing that the maiden must needs sit on the mossy bank and dabble her feet and her hands in it. While she was doing so, a ring slipped from her finger and before she could rescue it, was borne down the current and out of sight. The poor girl cried out in dismay, then fell to weeping so bitterly that her husband was astonished.

" Nay, now," said he soothingly, " truly

a paltry ring is not worth so many tears. My dearest, when I go again to my father's kingdom I will buy you a dozen rings more beautiful than that which you have lost! So dry your eyes and think no more about it."

But the girl refused to be comforted. "That ring," said she between her sobs, " is a magic one, and its loss will bring all manner of woe to us both."

Nor was she mistaken in this. The ring was borne along by the swift stream for a long distance and was finally washed ashore near the pleasure gardens of a great Khan. There some one found it and, seeing that it was a strange ring, curiously wrought, took it at once to the Khan himself. The monarch looked long upon it, and then, calling his ministers about him, he said:

" This trinket has magic power about it. I believe that it belongs to a very beautiful woman, perhaps the daughter of some king. Take it, therefore, and wheresoever it leads you, follow. And if its owner indeed proves to be a lovely damsel, take her prisoner and bring her at once to me, that she may be head over my household."

The chief minister bowed low, took the ring and called a goodly number of soldiers and servants to accompany him on his quest. As soon as he held the magic ring in his hand, he felt a strange power drawing him; and as he yielded to that power, it led him out of the pleasure gardens to the bank of the stream, and then up along the bank straight toward the log hut in the woods. And so, in a very short time, the Khan's minister and all his soldiers and servants were standing before the door of the little house where the Prince's son and his wife had been living so happily together, and were calling them to come out at once. They dared not disobey, and so the unhappy husband led forth the beautiful damsel, weeping as if her heart would break, and delivered her to the Khan's minister. She was taken away at

once, and the poor Prince's son was left
alone to grieve in his lonely little cabin.
The old foster-father and mother were so
stricken with sorrow that it seemed they
would die, yet neither did they nor the
Prince's son dare to do anything against
the commands of the great Khan.

Meanwhile the girl was led by the chief
minister to the monarch's palace. He was
delighted with her beauty and charm and
paid not the slightest heed to her tears or
prayers to be allowed to return to her husband. She was made chief of the royal
servants, must needs live in the palace
within constant call of the Khan, and there
seemed to be no possible hope of escape.
Days passed by, and her sorrow and longing for her husband became ever greater
instead of less, until she began to grow
pale and thin, and those about her feared
she would sicken and die. The Khan, too,
noticed the change in her and tried every
means in his power to cheer her, but all in
vain. At last he grew angry.

"This husband of hers," he cried, "is making the fairest of my servants sickly and plain. But if it is, indeed, longing for him that is eating the bloom off her cheeks, I will quickly remedy the matter!" And calling the court executioner, he whispered a few words in his ear. "There now!" said he later to the damsel, "when you know that your husband is dead and there is no use in wishing for him any longer, then perhaps you will forget him and learn to smile again."

In vain did the poor girl plead with the monarch for her husband's life! The more she wept and besought him, the more angry and determined he became.

So the executioner set out with a number of soldiers and, finding the log hut in the woods, dragged forth the Prince's son with little gentleness and took him afar off to a meadow in which was a dry, deserted well. Down in this the poor lad was thrust, and a great rock was rolled over it. There in the darkness he laid him down to die, with no hope of rescue and no desire for life, anyway, if he could not live it with his dear and beautiful wife.

Now it happened that the very next day was that on which the six friends had agreed to meet by the little round pond with the six streams running into it. And true to their promise, the other five gathered together and there awaited the coming of the Prince's son. The day passed slowly by and he did not appear, and then they noticed that the tree which he had planted was drooping and withering.

" Our friend is in danger or trouble," said the Doctor's son. " Let us lose no time in searching for him; even now we may be too late to save him." The others were alarmed at the ill omen and were eager to start at once, but the Magician's son detained them.

" One moment! " said he. " By my magic art I can learn exactly where our friend is, and then we can go straight to him." Bidding the others sit down and wait, he drew a circle on the ground and, placing himself in the center of it, began to recite all manner of incantations and to draw figures and signs in the air. After a while he erased the circle and announced to his friends that he knew the exact whereabouts of the Prince's son at that moment. " But we must hurry," he said, " for he is in great danger and will surely die unless we rescue him."

So the five set out at a smart pace and traveled all that night without pause or rest. By early morning they had reached the well wherein the Prince's son was imprisoned.

" How shall we move away the rock? " said they in despair, seeing the huge boulder completely covering the mouth of the well.

" I will move it! " said the Blacksmith's son, and taking the heavy iron hammer which he always carried in his belt, he fell to work upon the rock, knocking great

chunks out of it until it was all broken to
pieces.

When the mouth of the well had thus
been opened, they hastily lowered the Doctor's son, who found the son of the Prince
lying there quite white and still and nigh
unto death.

" It is well they chose me to fetch him
up! " he muttered as he drew forth his bag
of medicines. Taking a small flask of red
fluid, he poured the contents of it down the
throat of his unconscious friend, who soon
began to stir and then to sit up.

With great difficulty the two were
hauled up to the mouth of the well, and
when they were once safely out of it, the
friends all embraced with heartfelt joy and
affection. Then the Prince's son told the
tale of his adventure and its sorry ending,
and the other five were full of compassion
for him and indignation against the
wicked Khan.

" I have a plan! " suddenly spoke up
the Wood-carver's son. " By my art I can

fashion a great wooden bird, large enough to carry a man, and I will fit it with wings, hinges and springs so that it will fly through the air."

" And I," cried the Painter's son, catching the idea at once, " will paint and adorn it with marvellously beautiful colors, so that it will look like a Bird of Paradise."

They were all much excited by this time and prayed the Wood-carver's son to tell them more.

" Why, then," said he, " the Prince's son shall fly in my wonder bird to the palace of the Khan——"

" And when that wicked ruler sees the beauty and the color of it," interrupted the Painter's son, " he will go up to the roof to receive it, with all his royal household, and then — and then——"

" You can snatch up your wife and bear her away! " they all shouted at once to the Prince's son, who was fairly trembling with joy and hope.

The Wood-carver's son fell to work at

once, and in no time at all had built a marvellous wooden bird, big and strong and powerful, with great broad wings that would carry it through the air at the touch of a spring. Then the Painter's son got out his paints and adorned it with colors rich and fair, so that it shone with beauty like a true Bird of Paradise. The Prince's son got into it as soon as it was ready, and, amid the shouts of his friends, pressed a spring and flew high up into the air. Then off he steered, straight for the Khan's royal dwelling.

Great was the excitement at the palace when the big colored bird was seen flying overhead. Everybody rushed about, asking what it might mean, and the Khan was the most excited of them all.

" It is a Bird of Paradise! " he cried, " for see you not the gold upon its wings? It is, doubtless, bearing a messenger to me from the gods! In truth, we must meet him fittingly! " So he called together all his royal servants; choosing the wife of the

Prince's son because she was the fairest of all, he bade her go quickly to the roof and welcome the strange messenger as he alighted.

The damsel hastened to obey and stood waiting and marvelling as the great wooden monster drew near. Imagine her joy when it came whirring to a standstill, disclosing her own dear husband seated within it! In a flash he had caught her up and before the astonished Khan and his court could realize what was happening, the "Bird of Paradise" had left the palace roof far behind and was only a vanishing speck in the distance.

"And did they escape out of the country? And were the five faithful friends rewarded?" asked the Prince eagerly, as the Siddhi-kur ceased speaking.

"Indeed, yes!" said he, and he laughed merrily. "The Prince's son and his lovely wife, and old foster-father and mother, and the five companions all left

In a flash he had caught her up and had left the
palace roof far behind.   *Page 94.*

that country and went to live in a fair land, where they were all happy and prosperous to the end of their days!

"But see now, Prince, you have neglected again the command of Nagarguna, the wise master. You have opened your lips and broken silence on the homeward way, and so I am free again — as free as the wind in my mango tree beside the garden of ghost children!"

And with a shout the Siddhi-kur leaped from his bag and ran off, leaving the Khan's son looking disconsolately after him.

"The name of the tale which I shall tell you now," said the Siddhi-kur, "is 'The Secret of the Khan's Barber.'"

He was again upon the Prince's back, being borne along toward the dwelling of the great master, Nagarguna. The Prince nodded his head in sign of agreement, but he determined this time that no word should pass his lips, no matter how interested he might become in the story. So, settling down comfortably in his sack, the Siddhi-kur began.

TALE FOUR

THE SECRET OF THE KHAN'S BARBER

Once upon a time, long, long ago, there lived in the East a mighty Khan. He had broad, fertile lands to rule over and many thousands of faithful subjects, but though he governed wisely and well, the country was filled with discontent, and for a very good reason. Never did the Khan permit himself to be seen by his people, and he even obliged his courtiers and advisers to address him from behind tapestries and never allowed any of them to look upon his face. And this was not the worst, by any means. Every once in so often a youth was chosen from among the people, and was taken to the palace, where he was dressed in gorgeous attire, and then led into the presence of the Khan. There he was bidden to act as barber and cut the monarch's hair, and after he had done so he invariably disappeared and was never seen or heard of again. Of course, it was easy to guess that he had been put to death. Needless to say, the fathers and mothers of young men lived in constant dread and hated the Khan with their whole hearts, yet they had no power to withstand his orders.

Now it happened one day that the Khan's messenger stopped at the house of a widow who had only one child, — a fine, handsome lad whom she loved better than life itself. It had fallen to the lot of this youth, Daibang by name, to be the Khan's barber on the following day; but when the widow heard the news, instead of vainly weeping and complaining as others had done, she went at once to her kitchen, for she had devised a plan whereby her son might yet be saved. With great care she baked some little cakes of rice flour and milk, very light and fine and tempting to look upon, and into them she kneaded the great love that filled her heart for her son. Then calling him to her, she said:

" Daibang, on the morrow you must go to the palace to cut the Khan's hair, and after that, what fate may befall you we may not know, but we can very well guess. Then do exactly as I bid you, and my heart tells me you will escape the hard lot that has come to so many others. Take with you these cakes which I have baked for you with loving care, and while you are performing your duty to the Khan, manage to eat one of them so that he will see you do it. He will then ask to taste one himself, and when he has eaten of it he will wish to know what it is made of. Tell him that your mother made these cakes, of rice flour and milk, and that she kneaded into them her love and prayers for you. After that I think he will not find it in his heart to take your life."

Daibang accepted the cakes gratefully

and kissed his mother, and when the time came for him to go to the palace, he set forth with a light heart and high courage. Having arrived there, he was taken at once by servants and clad in rich clothing, then led into the presence of the Khan. With comb and scissors of pure gold, he dressed and cut the monarch's hair, and as he looked at him, he learned the Khan's secret and why it was that he allowed no one to look upon him and live; and Daibang's mind was filled with wonder. Nevertheless, he did not forget his mother's commands and managed to eat one of her cakes while he was combing the royal hair.

"What are you eating?" asked the Khan, and Daibang spread out his mother's cakes before him. They looked extremely good, and the monarch at once demanded one to eat. They tasted even better than they looked, and all the rest of the time Daibang was working over him the great Khan sat munching the cakes with evident enjoyment.

" Good youth," said he, at length, " tell me what these are made of, for I must have my royal cook learn the art and bake me such goodly cakes daily. Never have I tasted anything better."

" Sire," replied Daibang, " these are very simple cakes; they are made of rice flour and milk — my mother baked them and kneaded into them her love and prayers for me, her only child."

After that the Khan remained silent for a long time. When at last Daibang had finished his work and begged leave to retire, the Khan turned and, looking steadfastly at him, said:

" Young man, the love that your mother kneaded into those cakes has entered my very soul, and I cannot bring myself to give the order for your execution, as I have done these many times with lads like you. Nevertheless, you have learned my secret, and for that reason you should die, for I trust no man on earth, nor any woman either, to keep a secret entirely locked up in his own mind."

Daibang bowed low, but said nothing. After a moment the Khan continued:

"In truth, lad, my love for you grows, and I am minded even to trust your word and let you live. Will you promise, by your mother's love and by all else in this world that you consider holy, not to breathe to any man or any woman the secret concerning me that you have learned this day? And will you promise also to tell no one in what manner your life was spared?"

Solemnly and in all true faith Daibang knelt down and promised to keep stead-fastly these two things, as long as he lived. With that he was dismissed, and servants were ordered to load him with presents and conduct him home.

Great was the wonder of the people in the village when they learned that Daibang had returned unharmed from the palace, after having acted as the Khan's barber. They came in crowds to the widow's cottage and demanded eagerly how it was that he had escaped, and what the Khan's great secret was, anyway, that he should refuse at any time to be seen by his people, or to let those live who had once set eyes upon him. But to all their questions and wonderings Daibang said never a word. That night his mother, too, besought him to tell her just how he had fared and about the Khan's secret, but he only said to her:

" Mother mine, ask me no more. Your cakes worked the loving magic you foretold, and I have escaped death, but I have given my word of honor that I will tell no human being — not even my dear and faithful mother — the secret I learned while I was cutting the Khan's hair."

So the days and weeks and months passed by, and still every once in so often a fine young man would be chosen from among the people and taken to the palace to trim the Khan's hair, after which he

would be put to death. Not one escaped as
Daibang had done. And still the people
came to the widow's cottage and entreated
Daibang to tell them the monarch's secret.
Now he was a tender-hearted and a willing
youth, and he yearned most earnestly to
break his promise, more especially when
mothers and fathers besought him with
tears and prayers to tell them how he had
been spared, so that their sons might live
also.

At length, so great was the strain of the
secret on his mind and heart, that Daibang
grew very ill. Doctors came to him from
all parts of the country, and his mother
nursed him with tender care, day and
night, yet steadily he grew worse and
worse.

" The lad will die," the doctors said to
his mother; " he will surely die unless he
breathes forth the secret that is resting so
heavily upon his mind."

But Daibang remained faithful. " I
have promised," said he, " by my mother's

love and by all else that I call holy, to tell my secret to no living being, and I will die rather than break my word." So the doctors all departed, saying there was nothing further they could do.

That night the widow devised a plan. Sitting beside her son as he lay, restless and tossing on his bed, she said:

" Daibang, my child, hearken to me that you may live and not die. I have a plan whereby you may keep your promise to the Khan and yet rid your soul of its heavy secret. Take courage! hasten and get strong, then go forth alone into a far desert place. There find a hole in the ground, or a crevice in a rock, and when you have put your lips down close, speak out the whole matter that is weighing upon your heart. So shall you keep your promise and yet find relief for your soul and live."

This advice seemed good to Daibang, and so encouraged was he by the hope of ridding himself of his secret that he straightway began to mend. In a short time he had recovered strength enough to start forth and carry out the suggestion of his mother. He traveled many miles from home and came at length to a desert place full of rocks and sand, far from every sign of human dwelling. And in the middle of this waste land he found a deep, dark hole. Kneeling upon the ground, Daibang put his lips close to this hole and whispered all his secret. Three times he told it, and then he arose, feeling light-hearted again and well in body and mind.

Now it happened that in this hole lived a marmot, very old and clever, and he heard and understood Daibang's words, and knew it was the great Khan's secret he was telling. Being an idle, gossipy fellow, he repeated it all to his friend Echo, and as Echo always repeated everything he heard, whether secret or otherwise, he soon told the wind and the wind bore the Khan's secret far and wide over the land, and back at last into the palace garden, where the Khan himself was sitting. When the monarch heard the wind whispering about his secret, he was filled with rage.

"Truly," he said to himself, "the whole world must be talking about my secret if even the wind bandies it about! I did wrong to spare the life of that fellow Daibang, and to-morrow before sunrise he shall die!"

So it came about that Daibang was arrested that very day and dragged to the palace by rough soldiers. He was thrust at once into the private council room and there found himself alone with the angry Khan.

"Did I not say that no man on earth could keep a secret faithfully?" he cried sternly to the lad. "And you, though I loved and believed in you, have betrayed your trust, for the very wind that plays in my garden is whispering of that which none but you could tell! Speak, now, if you have aught to say in self-defense, for to-morrow, at daybreak, you shall die!"

Daibang had been frightened and confused by the rough handling of the soldiers, but now, hearing of what he was accused and knowing that he had done no wrong, he took courage and told the Khan honestly and without restraint all that he had done.

" Indeed, Sire," said he at the end, " no human being knows your secret even now, and it was only to save my life and because of the prayers of my mother that I spoke it into a hole in a desert place."

The Khan was touched by this story, his anger vanished, and he felt again the love in his heart for this faithful lad which he had felt first when he had eaten of his mother's cakes. They talked a long time together, and the end of it all was that Daibang was made the Khan's Chief Councilor, and he and his mother lived thereafter in high state and luxury at the royal palace.

You may be sure Daibang and his clever mother were not long in devising a way of hiding the Khan's secret so that he could go abroad among his people like other kings. And never again was a young man chosen to cut the Khan's hair and afterwards be put to death! That service Daibang kept for himself and remained the Lord High Royal Barber to the end of his days.

" But what *was* the Khan's secret? " demanded the Prince, when the Siddhi-kur had finished his tale.

" Oh, that," said the Siddhi-kur, " was very simple; haven't you guessed it yet? The Khan had ears that were large and pointed like the ears of an ass, and he was frightfully ashamed of them. But the widow made him a tall velvet cap with lappets that came down over them, and after that he felt perfectly comfortable about himself. Of course such caps became the style in the kingdom, and I believe they are worn in the East, in court circles, this very day!

" But I have tarried long enough! My heart yearns again for my mango tree in the cool grove beside the garden of ghost children. Farewell, O Prince! Since you have again broken silence on the homeward way, you have no longer any power to hold me! "

The shame and remorse of the Prince at having failed again were pitiful to see, but knowing that tears and self-accusation were of no avail, he turned around and set off at a smart pace after the disappearing form of the Siddhi-kur.

" I have a story in mind," said the Siddhi-kur, as he journeyed once more in the magic sack on the back of the Prince toward the cave of the master, Nagarguna, " a very ancient story of a king's son as faithful and wise as yourself, my friend. Come now, would you like me to tell it? "

The Prince nodded his head, resolving

within himself that on no account whatever would he open his lips this time to
comment on the story. So the Siddhi-kur
began at once.

TALE FIVE

Many, many years ago, there dwelt in a far country a Khan who was great and good and dearly loved by his people. Yet no one in all his kingdom loved or admired him so much as did his faithful wife and young son. Truly there never was a happier, more affectionate family. The three shared their joys and sorrows, their cares, their pleasures and their secrets, and indeed one was scarcely ever seen without the other two. Now the Khan and his family and the whole kingdom had in common one great sorrow; the country was watered by a clear, broad stream, and unless this flowed, full and strong, all the year, the land dried up, there was a great famine, and the people died of hunger and thirst. At the source of this river lived two serpent-gods, hideous monsters, and as evil as they were ugly, and every year these frightful creatures demanded a young man or maiden whom they might devour. Unless this desire was speedily fulfilled, they stopped the water at the head of the stream, it dried up and the people began to suffer and then die.

Many and many a time had the Khan and his counselors talked of the matter the whole night through, scheming, planning, wondering how they might save the young people of the land from this dreadful fate, but all to no avail. If the serpents did not get their yearly gift of precious human blood, the death of hundreds of men, women and children was the result. And so it seemed better for one young man or maid to die each year than that so many should perish.

The time had now come for this terrible sacrifice, and throughout the length and breadth of the land there was sorrow and anxiety. Fathers and mothers could scarce sleep for thinking that it might be the turn of their son or daughter to go to the head of the river and be cast into the cave of the monster serpents. Nowhere was there more unhappiness than in the family of the Khan, for he grieved for each lad or lass as if each were his own child. Seeing the care and sorrow in his father's face, the Khan's son, whose name, by the way, was Schalu, thought long and earnestly.

" Surely," he kept repeating to himself, " there must be *some* way in which I can help my father and free my country from this great curse! " But no matter how hard he thought, no way presented itself to his mind. The fateful time drew ever nearer, and finally the very next day was the dreaded one on which the serpent-gods would send a messenger, demanding by name some girl or boy in the kingdom.

That night Schalu could not sleep for

thinking of the tragedy of the morrow. "Suppose *I* were the one," he thought. " Of course they would not really dare to ask for the Khan's son — but just suppose —" and then he pictured to himself the sorrow of his father and mother and his own horror at such a death. " And we are no different, really, from the others," he said to himself. " The fathers and mothers among our subjects must suffer as keenly as their king and queen would, and as for the boys and girls — they are really just like me." All at once Schalu sat up in bed and stared into the darkness; a great idea had entered his mind.

" I will go to these terrible serpent monsters myself! " he breathed excitedly. " I will offer *myself* to them — I, a Khan's son — if they will give up their frightful practice hereafter! " There was little sleep for Schalu after he had made up his mind to this deed; all night long he lay wide awake, planning how he would plead and argue with the serpents for the lives of his people, and getting up his courage to meet his fate and die bravely, as befitted a prince.

Very early in the morning, before the sun was up, he arose, dressed himself and slipped quietly from the palace. He had not gone far before he was startled by hearing a step behind him, and turning around he saw Saran, a faithful friend, following him. Now Saran was a boy of his own age who had been brought up at the palace with him, as his servant and companion, and he and the Prince loved each other as brothers.

"O my master and friend!" said Saran, running up to Schalu. "Forgive me for having followed you! I have seen your trouble and anxiety these many days, and when you started forth alone this morning, my heart misgave me that some ill might befall you."

At first the Prince was much annoyed that he should have been discovered, but as he looked at Saran, he suddenly felt re-

lieved to have a friend near, and he opened
his heart and told all his plan of self-sac-
rifice. He feared Saran would entreat him
to give it up and go home, but his friend
listened in silence to the end and then said:

"Schalu, your heart is noble, as a
prince's should be! I cannot urge you to
give up a deed so truly glorious. Only I
beg you — and I will not be denied — let
me go with you and sacrifice myself also,
for life without you would be worse than
death, and mayhap if *two* of us give our
lives, the serpents will be the more willing
to leave our people in peace hereafter."

The Prince tried to dissuade his friend
but, seeing it was of no use, he soon
stopped, and the two lads continued on
their way together toward the head of the
stream.

As they approached the cave where the
serpents dwelt, they went slowly and
softly, for they were minded, if possible,
to get a good look at the monsters before
they allowed themselves to be seen. Creep-

ing up among the bushes by the side of the river they soon came to an opening through which they could peer, and there, seated on the bank, they saw the two horrible creatures. One was a long, thick, dragon-like being covered with scales of tarnished gold; the other was smaller and apparently younger, and the scales on its back were as green as emeralds. They had neither seen nor heard the two lads, and in a moment the golden one began to speak.

" It is strange, Brother," said he, " that these people are so ignorant and so faithful."

" They cannot very well help themselves, can they? " said the smaller, green one. "They know that if they fail in this sacrifice, we will dry up their stream, and then they will all perish."

" True," replied the other, " but after all, it would be so easy to kill us, you know, if they only knew how."

" But have they not sent armed soldiers

against us in times past? " said the green serpent, drawing himself up proudly; " and have we not routed them all and slain them? "

" Of course *swords* could not hurt us," said the golden one contemptuously, " but if they only knew enough to come out against us with thick, oak staves! One well-aimed blow on the head from such a weapon would finish us. But, luckily, they don't know that! "

" And are far too stupid ever to guess it, so we are perfectly safe," added the green one.

" And then," chuckled the big golden monster, writhing the folds of his long body comfortably about him. " To think what a man would gain by killing us! My head, cooked and eaten, would not only make a delicious meal, but it would give the eater power to pour forth gold from his mouth whenever he wanted to! "

" And if any one ate *my* head," said the green one, also chuckling, " emeralds would come from his mouth whenever he so desired. Lucky the stupid mortals will never know ! "

Schalu and his friend had heard enough. Trembling with excitement, they crept away from their hiding place, out of sound and sight of the serpents, and then fell to hugging each other for very joy of their discovery. They lost no time in making for themselves huge oak staves, and armed with these, they walked back to where the serpents still sat lazily talking together on the bank of the stream. With a shout, they leaped from the bushes upon the unsuspecting monsters and attacked them. The fight was short and sharp. The great creatures turned upon the two boys viciously and lunged at them with their hard, metallic heads, but the lads dodged skilfully and brought down blow after blow upon their enemies until at last they lay motionless and quite dead.

" Now," said Prince Schalu, leaning on his staff and breathing hard, " we must build a fire and cook ourselves a meal, and if the serpent-gods spoke the truth, we shall then be rich for the rest of our lives."

With their knives they cut off the heads of their dreaded enemies and, having built a fire of twigs, they cooked them well and then ate them. Schalu ate the golden head and declared it delicious, while Saran said that he had never tasted anything quite so good as the emerald-green head.

" Let us see," said the Prince, when they had finished, " how well the charm works. I wish that my mouth would pour forth gold!" Scarcely had he finished speaking before a rain of bright gold coins fell from his lips, and the boys gathered them up in big handfuls and stowed them away in their pockets.

"Now let me try!" said Saran. " I wish that my mouth would pour forth emeralds!" Immediately emeralds pattered to the ground in great profusion.

"What fun!" said Saran, gathering them up. " Now let us hasten back to the palace and show your royal father all that we have accomplished!"

"No, don't let us go home yet," said the Prince. "One adventure is but a stepping-stone to another, and I am minded to travel a bit and see what fortune we may meet by the way. With this marvellous gift of gold and emeralds, we should surely come by some strange and interesting experiences."

To this plan Saran readily agreed; the two set forth with merry hearts and, finding an unfamiliar road, followed it, they knew not whither. All day long they traveled, meeting many wayfarers, but finding nothing in the shape of an adventure. In the late afternoon they reached a palm grove whence came shouts and cries and signs of great commotion. Hurrying toward the scene of disturbance, they beheld half a dozen lusty boys fighting most brutally.

"Here, young fellows!" cried the Prince, "stop that at once and tell us what

you are fighting about!" But the boys
paid no heed to him at all.

"Stop!" cried Schalu again, shouting
to make himself heard above the din.
"Stop, and I will show you a marvel the
like of which you have never seen!"

Hearing this, the boys ceased fighting
on the instant, and all turned and stared
at Schalu and Saran.

"Marvel, did you say?" exclaimed the
leader scornfully. "You can't show us a
marvel greater than the one we have got
right here!"

"Have you something wonderful,
too?" asked the Prince. "Well, then, let
us make a bargain; if my marvel is greater
than yours, you shall give me yours, and if
yours is greater than mine, I will give you
each as much gold as two hands can
carry."

"Hurrah!" cried the boys, delighted.
"Let us do it!" They all gathered
around in a circle, while their leader
picked up from the ground a torn and bat-

tered cap. "This," said he, "is what we were fighting about, for each of us wants it for himself. This is a magic cap, and whoever puts it on remains invisible until he takes it off again. Show us a marvel equal to *that*, if you can!"

Softly uttering a wish for gold, the Prince opened his mouth and immediately a great rain of coins tumbled to the ground. The boys fell upon them greedily, shouting, snatching and fighting.

"Come," said Schalu to his friend, "these boys are not worthy of owning such a treasure as the cap, and besides, my marvel is greater than theirs, so I am entitled to it."

He caught up the ragged cap, put it on his head and grasped Saran's hand. Straightway they both became invisible, and so passed through the midst of the fighting boys unnoticed and continued on their way.

"This is a prize well worth having!" said the Prince, after they had walked awhile and, taking the cap off, he hid it carefully in his bosom. "Now I wonder what our next adventure will be."

They had not gone far before they came to a cross-roads where there was a great cloud of dust and, hearing shouts and angry words, they hastened to see what it all meant. In the midst of the dust were half a dozen ugly dwarfs, fighting furiously, screaming and cursing each other.

"You try your hand at this!" said Schalu to his friend. "This shall be your adventure." So Saran stamped upon the ground and called out "Stop!" in a loud voice, but the dwarfs paid no attention to him at all. "Stop, I say!" he repeated louder than before. "I have a great marvel to show you!" At the word "marvel" the fighters ceased at once and stood staring at the two friends.

"Marvel, did you say?" exclaimed the leader. "Pooh! I don't care how wonderful it is, it can't be as great as ours!"

"What is yours?" said Saran. "If it

is as interesting as mine, you shall each have as many emeralds as your two hands can carry." At that all the dwarfs began to laugh scornfully.

"Show him! Show him!" they cried to their leader, "and then we will rob him of all his emeralds if, in truth, he has any."

The leader turned and picked up a pair of old, shabby-looking boots. "These," he said, "are magic, and if anybody puts even one of them on and makes a wish to be in any place under the sun, he will find himself there in the twinkling of an eye."

"That is indeed wonderful!" said Saran, "and here is your pay, but, in sooth, you deserve neither boots nor emeralds!" Then, to the great astonishment of the little men, Saran, uttering a wish for emeralds, opened his mouth and poured them forth, a great stream of glorious green gems. With a shout the dwarfs snatched them up, pushing and tearing them from each other.

"Quick!" said Saran to the Prince.

"Put on your cap and take my hand, so that they will not see us! We can make better use of the magic boots than these wicked dwarfs can." So they each hastily slipped on a boot and, being invisible because of the magic cap, passed out from among the dwarfs before they had stopped fighting over the jewels.

"And now," said Saran, "while we have on the boots, let us test their power by wishing to be somewhere."

"Very well," said Schalu, "I wish that we may be taken at once to a country that needs a king!"

Immediately the two friends felt themselves picked up and whizzed through the air with such speed that they could see nothing and feel nothing but the wind rushing by their ears. Then they were put down gently upon the ground and found themselves in a strange country.

Soon they saw a great procession of men, women and children advancing toward them, and at their head walked an old man with snowy beard and hair and clad in long white garments. The people came straight up to the Prince and Saran, and there halted, while the old man addressed them in eager, trembling tones.

"You are strangers," said he, "and we are seeking strangers; I pray you, can you show us some magic sign whereby we may know that you are not as other mortals are?"

"Indeed," said Prince Schalu, "we are no different from other men, but by great good fortune we have this day become possessed of several wonders."

"Show us! Show us!" cried the crowd in great excitement.

"This," continued Schalu, drawing the battered magic cap from his pocket, "has the power of making its wearer invisible." He put it on, and the people cried out in wonder and anxiety, "Where are they? Where are they? They are gone! Find them! They are truly the ones!"

"No, we are still here," said the Prince,

removing the cap. " But why does it matter so much to you? And why are you so anxious to see our marvels? "

" Show us more! Show us more! " the crowd shouted, and the old man in white tried vainly to quiet them, for he was as much excited as they.

" These boots," Schalu went on, pointing to the magic ones, " are also very wonderful, for they will bear us wheresoever we wish to be in the twinkling of an eye. It was by their means that we came here."

" Don't try them! We'll believe you! " cried somebody, as if fearful of losing them, and the crowd surged eagerly forward again.

" And finally," said Schalu, smiling at them and thoroughly enjoying their wonder, " my friend and I have a little trick which may interest you." Opening their mouths, the two began to pour forth gold and emeralds and toss them in great handfuls among the crowd.

If they were excited before, the people

now went mad with surprise and joy, and while they were grasping at the precious things, the old, white-haired man approached Schalu and said:

" O marvellous stranger, know that I am a magician, and by my art I learned that this land which has been without a king for many a long day would find a just, wise and righteous ruler in a wonder-working stranger whom we should meet traveling along this road to-day. Accept, then, our kingdom; come and rule over our people, and we will honor you as our Khan and your companion as Grand Vizier to the end of our days! "

The crowd had by this time grown silent, listening, and at the end of the speech they set up a shout that echoed to the very clouds. Seizing Schalu and Saran in their arms, they bore them with laughter and singing to the palace, where Schalu was crowned with all pomp and ceremony, and Saran was made his chief adviser.

And so the two friends lived worthily and happily till the end of their days.

The tale being finished, the Siddhi-kur was silent.

"But what of the poor father and mother?" exclaimed the Prince impatiently. "Surely Schalu was a faithless son if he left his parents to die of grief for him!"

"Dear me, no! He didn't do that!" said the Siddhi-kur, smiling. "He was no sooner made king than he journeyed back to visit his royal father and mother, and I leave you to imagine their joy and the happiness of the whole land when it became known that the prince and his faithful friend had not only returned in safety, but had delivered them from the curse of the serpent-gods and had won, besides, such glory and riches.

"But I fear me!" continued the Siddhi-kur, playfully poking the Khan's son in the ribs, "that *you* will never attain glory and riches, unless you remember the words of Nagarguna and keep silent on your homeward way! Farewell — I am off to my mango tree, and it is good indeed to be free again!"

The Prince could scarcely keep back his tears of anger and vexation as he watched the Siddhi-kur skipping gayly off to the north.

" I will fetch you yet!" he cried, but the magic creature only turned and smiled at him indulgently.

" I would give it up, if I were you," said he; " but if you really are determined to get me again, I've a nice story to tell you on the way back, — ' The Strange Adventure of Schalu's Wife.' " With that he ran on and disappeared in the distance.

TALE SIX

For several years Schalu reigned over his new-found kingdom, quietly, wisely and well, ably advised and assisted by his faithful friend, Saran. His people loved him, and there was happiness and prosperity throughout the land. One day a group of men stood without the council chamber and begged an audience with the Khan. Schalu graciously admitted them and asked what it was they desired.

" Sire," said they, " we are come from the people to ask you a boon, not so much for ourselves as for your Majesty. These many years you have been with us, and yet you have not taken unto yourself a wife, and we wish mightily that you would wed some princess and so fill your home with happiness, and perchance give us a son to love and look to as our future ruler."

This saying pleased the Khan, and he inquired about all the princesses in nearby kingdoms, declaring that he would set about at once choosing a royal wife. After that he spent many days visiting other countries and meeting princesses and great ladies from far and near; but not one of these lovely maidens entirely pleased him or made him feel that she alone out of all the world was the one for him. This damsel had a voice too sharp; that one's temper was too quick; the other seemed cold and indifferent, — and so it was. Day after day the people expected tidings of a royal marriage, and day after day, with keen disappointment, they watched the Khan ride back to his palace alone and dejected.

At last, when Schalu was returning after

another fruitless journey into a far land
to visit a lady of great renown, he happened to pass a small house on the outskirts of his kingdom. And standing in
the doorway was the most beautiful damsel his eyes had ever looked on. She was
tall and slim, with long, black hair reach-
ing almost to her ankles. Her eyes were
big and black as midnight, and her lips
were red. Moreover, there was a soft
magic in her face, a something so lovely
that the Khan stood spellbound, gazing at
her in silence for a long time. Then, all
at once, he realized that this cottage girl, in
her simple work-a-day frock, was the one
woman in all the world that he wanted for
his wife. No more looking about for
princesses and grand ladies! He had
found what he longed for, and he would
make this damsel his queen.

The matter was soon settled, for was not
the Khan's word law in the land? A great
marriage feast was held in the palace, holi-
days were proclaimed throughout the land

and there were revelry and mad rejoicing among all the people. If there were any to murmur against the lowliness of the new queen, their voices were quickly drowned by shouts of approval from those who had been fortunate enough to look at the beautiful face of the bride, and when the days of festivity were over, everybody settled down in peace and contentment, feeling that their Khan was at last to have a happy home life.

But it was far otherwise. Though Schalu loved his queen with all his heart, though he showered riches and treasures upon her, and though he racked his brain to find amusements and pleasures to make her happy, she only looked upon him coldly and strangely and grew ever paler, quieter and apparently more sorrowful every day. In vain the Khan besought her to tell him what he could do to please her and to win her love; in vain he tried to find out whether she had any secret cause of woe, — he could do nothing. And day by day he became more disappointed and unhappy. It grieved the courtiers and the people to see this, but above all it grieved Saran, his faithful friend, until at last he could stand it no longer and, going to Schalu, he said:

" My dear Master, my heart is nigh dead within me to see you, the best of men and of monarchs, so sorrowful. I pray you, let me advise you! It seems to me, Sire, that the queen must bear some hidden grief in her heart, else she would surely give you her love. Perhaps, if we could discover what her trouble is, we could cure it and make her the loving wife you so desire."

" Saran, my friend," said the Khan wearily, " have I not tried every means in my power to win the queen's love and confidence — and all to no avail? "

" Then let me try," said Saran eagerly, " for my heart tells me I shall succeed even where my royal master has failed."

" Very well," said Schalu, but he spoke without hope or interest.

From that moment, wearing the " invisible " cap, Saran watched the queen day
and night, unknown to her. He neglected
food and sleep that he might follow her
continually, but she gave no hint at any
time, by word, look or deed, of any hidden
cause of sorrow. Saran was about to give
up in despair when, one evening, he
noticed a peculiar restlessness in the lady.
She looked often at the sky, moved un-
easily about the palace and seemed in an
absent, dreamy state of mind. At last she
retired to her own rooms, soon to emerge
dressed in a long black mantle and hood
which hid her face almost completely.
Silently, and with many an uneasy look
behind her, she made her way to a small,
seldom used, back gate in the palace
garden and thence out into the highroad.
Once there, she vanished in the twinkling
of an eye, and Saran, looking frantically
in all directions, could find no trace of her.
He dashed back into the palace, seized the

magic boots from their hiding-place,
tugged them on and muttered his wish:

"Take me wherever the queen is!"

For a moment the wind sang in his ears
and the stars sped by him; then he found
himself on earth again and walking in a
beautiful, strange garden. Never had he
smelled such fragrance or seen such profusion of flowers as these that were dimly
visible in the moonlight! Paths led in
many directions between rows of gorgeous
bloom, and down one of them he could
make out the faint outline of the queen in
her long, black robe. He went on quickly
and silently. She approached a palace
which stood at the end of the garden, entered through a small gate, and hurried
along a short, narrow passageway into an
open court. Saran followed, still wearing
the magic cap, and soon found himself in
a brilliantly lighted room, rich beyond
words and filled with a soft, smoky incense
which rose in clouds from a brazier standing in a corner. So interested was he in

looking about him that he quite forgot the queen for a moment and was astonished to see her step forth into the light, clad, not in her long, dark robe, but in flame-colored silk, embroidered with gold and precious stones. She approached the brazier and waved her arms slowly over it, muttering strange words in a hard, monotonous voice. Scarcely had she ceased speaking and dropped her hands to her side when in through the window flew a bird of gorgeous plumage. It darted three times through the smoke of the incense and then disappeared in a flash of light, and in its place appeared a tall, handsome man, dressed in rich garments like a prince. He looked angrily at the queen, who still stood gazing at the brazier, nor did she even glance at him as he said:

" Have you done as I bade you? "

She shook her head.

" What? " said he, stamping his foot. " After all my careful teaching, does the Khan still keep his natural form and the power of pouring gold from his mouth? Have I not given you fame and wealth and taught you magic only upon condition that you would destroy your husband?"

The unhappy queen covered her face with her hands. "I cannot do it!" she whispered. "Transform the Khan into a dog and take from him all his magic powers! I cannot, cannot do it!"

"And why not, pray?" asked the strange man with a mocking laugh. "You do not love the Khan! I have, by my magic, made that impossible."

Saran, watching and listening from a near corner, let slip an exclamation of wonder. "So that is it!" he thought. "She is kept from loving her husband by wicked magic!"

Both the queen and the stranger started at the sound, but on looking around, could see nothing, for Saran, of course, still wore his "invisible" cap.

"Enough of this!" cried the man at length, after he had waited in vain for the queen to answer his question. "To-morrow I will take matters into my own hands. In the form of a snake I will seek the Khan and cast a spell upon him. Thereafter he will be completely in my power."

The queen turned toward him imploringly, but like a flash he had changed himself into a bird again and was gone through the open window.

Slowly and sorrowfully the queen turned away from the glowing brazier, caught up her black robe and put it over her shoulders. As Saran followed her out to the beautiful garden, he could hear her softly crying, and his heart grew big with pity for her and anger at the strange man whom he now knew to be a wicked demon.

The next day Saran ordered a great fire to be built in the council hall, and he bade Schalu and his queen sit before it. While they were so doing, into the hall crept a great ugly serpent, green and slimy and loathsome to look on. He raised his head high and fastened his evil eyes upon

Schalu, and the Khan became white and motionless and looked like one dead. The snake swayed to and fro, muttering strange words, but before his spell was ended, Saran had fallen upon him and was beating his head with a huge staff. Then the serpent turned and attacked Saran, and mightily they fought together at the edge of the great fire. Sometimes Saran would nigh fall into the flames, and sometimes the wicked demon, and great was the noise of their cries and shouting. At last the great serpent made a sudden, unexpected turn, glided under Saran's arm and plunged at Schalu. In one breathless moment he would have reached him, but with a cry the queen jumped forward, cast her arms around the snake's hideous green neck and flung him from her into the fire. A great smoke arose, and with a scream an ugly demon leaped from the midst of the flames and flew out through the window, leaving his snake form behind him, smoldering in the ashes!

" My! " exclaimed the Prince, standing still in excitement. " How thrilling! And did Schalu recover from his spell, and did the brave queen love him after that? "

" Yes, indeed! " said the Siddhi-kur with a little laugh. " The wicked demon lost all his power over the queen after that and never troubled her or her husband again. And she proved to be a most loving and dutiful wife, and they all lived happily together for the rest of their days."

" Saran should have had a lovely wife, too," said the Prince thoughtfully, beginning to move on again.

" Wait a bit, my friend," said the Siddhi-kur, " you may add to the story as you wish, by yourself, as you journey onward! As for me, I am off for the cool grove beside the garden of ghost children, for you have broken silence again on your way home, and I am free once more! "

With a shout of joy he leaped from the magic sack and dashed off toward the

north, where his mango tree stood awaiting him.

The Prince sighed wearily. "Oh, how
stupid I am!" said he. "But I will get
the Siddhi-kur even yet, and carry him to
my master, Nagarguna, if I have to spend
the rest of my life in doing it!"

And so it came about that in a few days
the Khan's son was again journeying back
toward the cave of Nagarguna bearing
upon his back the Siddhi-kur.

"Friend," said that creature of magic,
at length. "I have just bethought me of
a marvellous tale which I am minded to
tell you. You may listen or not, as
you wish; for me, at least, it will make
the way and the hours seem shorter. The
name of this story is 'The Fortunes of
Shrikantha.'"

TALE SEVEN

THE FORTUNES OF SHRIKANTHA

There was once a lad, the son of a Brahman, who was neither very poor nor very rich, very good nor very bad, very wise nor very foolish, but who had the kindest heart in all the world. His name was Shrikantha, and he lived long ago in India. When he was old enough to do as he liked, he sold all that he had and bought three pieces of cloth goods, very fine and handsome, and with these he was minded to trade and make his fortune. He bade his parents good-by and started forth to journey to a near-by city where he thought he might trade to the best advantage.

He had not gone far before he came upon a band of cruel boys who were tormenting a little mouse.

"Stop!" said Shrikantha, in anger.

" The mouse is suffering and will die! Have you no pity in your hearts? " But the boys only laughed at him and continued their wicked play. So, seeing that words were useless, Shrikantha bargained with them, and they finally agreed to set the mouse free in return for one of his three handsome pieces of cloth. After he had seen the little creature scamper safely away, Shrikantha sighed and continued his journey, the poorer by one third of his possessions, but with a satisfied heart.

A little farther on, what should he see but another group of boys ill treating an ape and laughing to see the poor thing suffer. Shrikantha tried to hurry by without noticing it, but he could not endure to see pain and do nothing to relieve it, so in a moment he stopped and tried by reasoning with the boys to make them cease their cruelty. As in the first case, he found his words were all in vain, and only by giving up his second piece of goods could he buy relief and freedom for the ape. And now he felt poor indeed, having nothing left in the world save one handsome bit of cloth.

"Never mind," said he to himself reassuringly, "even with this, if I bargain shrewdly, I may trade and make my fortune. At any rate, the look of gratitude that poor ape gave me was worth much more than a paltry piece of merchandise." So he went on with a light step and a merry heart, but, to his dismay, he soon heard again a cry of pain and saw yet another group of boys gathered around a young bear and cruelly abusing it.

"Alas!" thought Shrikantha. "This time I must harden my heart and pass by, for well I know words will do no good, and I cannot give away my last possession!" He quickened his step and tried to think of something else as he hurried by, but at that moment the poor little bear cried out so piteously that he could not endure it. Turning about, he hastened to where the

unkind lads were standing and spoke long
and earnestly with them. But, as it had
been in the two other cases, so it was now;
Shrikantha argued in vain and finally had
to offer his last treasure that the bear might
go free. Then he started forth again
empty-handed.

" I might as well go back to my father,"
he thought, " yet not so — he will but
chide me for foolish kindness of heart! I
will continue on my way, for surely Dame
Fortune will repay me for what I have lost
in so good a cause!" Fortune, however,
was minded to do otherwise.

Now the road to the city led Shrikantha
directly by the palace of the Khan, and
just as he was passing the great gate, he
heard shouts and confusion within and
immediately a man dashed out.

" Run! Run for your life!" he cried,
as he rushed past, and Shrikantha, without stopping to think, did as he was told.

He heard the roar of many voices and
the running steps of many feet behind

him, and so he ran faster than ever. On and on he sped, but his pursuers slowly gained on him until he could hear their cries and curses, and even feel the panting breath of the foremost ones.

" Stop, thief! " they cried. " Stop the wicked thief! He has stolen the Khan's jewels! "

Hearing this, Shrikantha grew more alarmed and, instead of stopping at once to reason with the men that it was not he who had stolen the jewels, but doubtless the man ahead of him, he foolishly ran on faster than ever. At last his breath gave out completely, his knees seemed to break beneath him and he fell, panting and sobbing, to the ground. In a moment his pursuers were upon him and were binding him with a tight cord, kicking and abusing him between their gasping breaths. In vain did he try now to explain himself; he was too breathless to complete a single sentence, and they were too angry and too sure of their prey to listen. He was taken

at once to the Khan's court, and though
of course no jewels were found on him,
and though he pleaded his innocence with
tears and prayers, he was condemned to
die a horrible death. On the morrow, two
strong, cruel men threw him into a great
wooden chest, sealed the lid of it tight and
cast it into the river.

Poor Shrikantha felt the lapping of the
water against his air-tight box and gave
himself up as one already killed by cruel
fate. But Fate thought otherwise!

In a short time the great chest, bumping
along with the current of the river, caught
against some rocks on an island and there
stuck fast. And who should be on that
very spot but the little mouse whom
Shrikantha had saved from the abuse of
the cruel boys. Seeing the big, ungainly
box come a-shore on her island, the mouse
investigated the matter and soon discovered that her friend and rescuer was shut
up within.

" Have courage! " she squeaked to him,

through the cracks of the chest, and immediately she began to gnaw at a corner of it. When she had eaten out a hole in the wood large enough to admit some air to Shrikantha, who was already almost suffocated, she hurried off to find the ape and the bear. They soon returned with her, declaring they were only too glad to help. Together they dragged the chest a-shore, broke it open and set Shrikantha free. Then, for many days the three faithful creatures supplied the lad with nuts and fruits so that he suffered not at all for lack of food and drink.

One day the mouse came to Shrikantha, bearing in her mouth a small, blue stone.

"Take this, Master," said she, laying it in his hand. "It is a talisman, my dearest possession, and I give it to you in gratitude for what you did once upon a time for me. Take it and breathe a wish upon it, and you shall have your heart's desire."

Shrikantha looked at the little blue stone in wonder and, thinking that he would

Together they dragged the chest ashore and set
Shrikantha free. *Page* 152.

merely test its power, wished himself away
from the island. No sooner thought than
the island vanished beneath him, and he
found himself in a meadow on the mainland. He was surprised and delighted beyond words, and he looked at the blue
stone again and wished eagerly for a palace set in the midst of a beautiful park,
with rare trees, birds and flowers about it
and every luxury and comfort within. He
closed his eyes and, opening them again
in a moment, beheld a lovely garden where
the meadow had been, a gorgeous palace
in the distance, and all exactly as he had
wished to have it, only more beautiful and
wonderful than he had dared to think.
With the greatest joy he walked about his
park and into his palace, finding there
room after room richly furnished, servants bowing before him at every turn and
costly possessions strewn about in profusion. Truly, he thought to himself, a
Khan might now envy him his wealth!

"But I must have my faithful friends

here to enjoy all this good fortune with me!" said he to himself at length. So he wished for the mouse, the ape and the bear, and instantly they stood before him.

And now Shrikantha lived in luxury and happiness for some time, and it seemed as if he might continue to live so until the end of his days. But Fate planned otherwise. There came to the palace one day a caravan of wicked, thieving merchants, and the chief among them made friends with Shrikantha and in an evil moment persuaded him to tell the secret of his good fortune.

"Alas!" said the merchant, when Shrikantha had told him all and shown him the precious blue talisman. "How lucky some men are, how unlucky others! Here are you, scarcely more than a lad; you have never worked or traded or done anything whereby a man earns wealth, and yet you are loaded with every blessing, while I, who have toiled hard and honestly my whole life through, have nothing —

nothing in all the world but a handful of
cheap goods which I must bargain hard
to trade off for the bare necessities of my
miserable existence!" And with that he
sighed so wretchedly that Shrikantha's
tender heart melted within him.

"If only — " said the wicked merchant,
"but I must not suggest such a thing!"

"Suggest what?" asked Shrikantha,
full of sympathy.

"If only," continued the other, "if only
in the kindness of your heart, you would
lend me your talisman for one moment, I
could wish myself a comfortable little
home, and peace and quiet for the rest of
my days! You would be none the poorer;
indeed, you would be richer for the
prayers and blessings of a happy man!"

It was such a simple way in which to
help the poor fellow that Shrikantha did
not hesitate an instant, but put the magic
blue stone trustingly into his hands. With
a scornful laugh, the wicked merchant
shouted his wish aloud:

"I want all the possessions Shrikantha has, and I desire him to return to the place and state in which he was when this talisman was given to him!"

In a flash, Shrikantha found himself again on the island in the river, with not a sign of all his former wealth and glory about him. He sat down on the ground and beat his forehead with his hands.

"What a miserable fool I have been!" said he to himself, over and over again.

"Yes, you have been foolish, Master!" said a squeaky little voice in his ear, "but truly in kindness have you been so." Looking around, Shrikantha saw his friend, the little mouse.

"Of what avail is it that my heart is kind, if by that very kindness I lose everything I have in the world?" said he with a sigh, refusing to be comforted.

"You have not lost everything," corrected the mouse, "you still have three faithful friends who were won to you forever by that same kind heart of yours."

And without another word the little creature disappeared, leaving Shrikantha still lamenting on the ground.

It were too long a tale to tell how the three animal friends met and planned together, how they went at night to the palace of the wicked merchant, crept to his room, and how the ape and the bear waited breathlessly outside while the mouse climbed through the keyhole and stole the talisman from the breast of the sleeping man. They had little trouble in passing the many guards, who were on the lookout for men, not animals, to steal their master's treasure. When they reached the river, however, in sight of Shrikantha himself, a sorry adventure befell them. The bear was the only one of the three who could swim, and so, in order to cross the water, the ape got upon the bear's back, put the mouse upon his shoulder and the talisman in his mouth. Thus, with this precious, heavy load on his back, the bear started bravely on his long swim across to the island. In the very middle of the stream, a fish passed within a few feet of his nose, and he, foolish creature, made a dive for it. The ape lost his balance and cried out in fright, letting the blue talisman slip from his mouth into the water. Down it sank into the muddy depths, and the three friends, in dismay, watched it disappear.

" Alack-a-day! " wailed the little mouse. " We have spent all our time and labor for nothing, and our poor friend on the island will surely die of hunger and despair! What shall we do? Whatever *shall* we do? "

The bear turned and swam back to the mainland, and there the three sat down disconsolately on the shore.

" What a fool you were to jump at that fish! " said the ape to the bear crossly.

" What a fool *you* were not to keep your mouth shut, when you had such a treasure inside it! " growled the bear.

" Now don't waste time blaming each

other!" counselled the mouse. "It doesn't matter whose fault it was; the talisman is gone, and we must get it again; that is the thing to think about."

"Get it again!" the bear was crosser than ever. "I'd like to know how that can be done! It has gone to the bottom of the river, thanks to the carelessness of the ape, and we can never recover it. Let us go to our homes; we have done enough for the man already to more than pay for his kindness to us."

"Yes, let us go home," agreed the ape. "There is no use trying to do anything if the bear has to chase every fish he meets, regardless of the importance of his mission. And we have done enough for the man as it is."

"Don't, *don't* talk like that!" cried the little mouse. "You both know as well as I that we can never repay the man's kindness to us! Come, let us plan! There must be a way!" She walked up and down

the shore, thinking. " I have it! " she cried
at last.

" What? " said both the others, interested in spite of themselves.

" You watch me and do just as I tell
you," said she, and began crying in a loud
voice and running to and fro upon the
river bank.

At the sound of her outcry, the frogs
that live at the bottom of the river came to
the surface to learn what the matter was.
When a great crowd of them had collected,
the little mouse called out:

" Quick, friends, quick! Before it is
too late! The pebbles on your river bed
have been cursed, and the curse is about
to fall upon you! We have come to your
aid. Hand us all the pebbles at the bottom
of the river, and we will throw them all
away. Hurry and do as we bid you! "

The frogs, who were a silly, credulous
people, hastened to do as the mouse told
them. Diving down to the river bottom
they fetched the pebbles, one after another,

and handed them to their supposed pre-
server, who gave them to the ape and the
bear, bidding them fling the cursed things
away. More and more frogs gathered for
the task and brought up stones in countless numbers. At last one came, bringing
the precious, blue talisman, and when the
little mouse had got hold of it, she sig-
nalled to her friends to stop their work.
With a gesture, she made the frogs stand
still and in a solemn voice she cried:

"It is enough! The curse is lifted from
the river and its people! You have worked
well and saved yourselves (and us) much
sorrow. Go now and live in peace!"

The frogs murmured among themselves, being much puzzled by the whole
performance, but the bear, the ape and the
little mouse paused not to listen. Quickly
they started across the river, the ape on the
bear's back, the little mouse, still clutching
the talisman, on the shoulder of the ape.
In this manner they reached the island in
safety and there they found——

The Siddhi-kur paused and bit into a mango which he had brought with him, munching in silence for some time.

" Found *what?* " cried the Khan's son, standing still to wonder. " *I* know! He found that Shrikantha was already dead with hunger, having waited so long for his friends! "

" No, not at all! " said the Siddhi-kur. " Nothing of the sort! Shrikantha was sitting on the shore, patiently awaiting the return of his friends. As soon as the mouse had handed him the magic blue stone, he wished back all the good things he had had before and a wise and beautiful wife to enjoy it all with him. And you may be sure the lady took charge of the talisman as soon as they were married, so there was no danger of their losing their fortune again, as poor, foolish, kind-hearted Shrikantha had lost it before.

" However, if the Prince wishes my story to end otherwise, he may finish it to suit himself. Meanwhile, since he has again broken silence on the homeward way, I will leave him to meditate upon the story, his own lack of wisdom, or whatever he likes. As for me, I will hie me back to my mango tree in the cool grove beside the garden of ghost children!"

So the Siddhi-kur, with a joyful shout, leaped from the Prince's back and sped away again to the northward.

The Khan's son neither sighed nor lamented, but, setting his teeth grimly, he turned about and started forth once more after the magic creature, eating his cake which grew not less as he trudged along.

When the long journey to the north had been completed, and the Siddhi-kur had been called again from his mango tree and settled upon the back of the Prince, he began at once:

" I have a story in mind which is perhaps more strange and interesting than any I have yet told you. Listen, my friend, and I will begin it."

TALE EIGHT

SUNSHINE AND MOONSHINE

Long years ago, there lived in a distant land a good and handsome prince named Sunshine. He dwelt in a splendid palace with his father, who was a Khan, his stepmother and his stepbrother, whose name was Moonshine. His father and brother loved him dearly, but his stepmother hated him, being jealous for her own son, Moonshine. So, while the two boys lived happily together, never suspecting ill, this wicked woman plotted and schemed to destroy the life of Sunshine and so make her son heir to the throne.

At last, one day, she thought of a plan. Going to her room, she lay down, groaning and crying out as if she were ill and

in frightful pain. The Khan was soon
notified and was much alarmed when he
found the queen apparently in such a bad
condition.

" My dear wife," he cried, " I will have
the court physician summoned at once,
that he may give you a remedy."

" Nay," said the queen feebly, " it will
do no good. Already I am nigh unto
death, and none can help me. I am dying,
my Khan — I am dying fast, and the one
and only remedy for my sickness I can
never have."

" One remedy? " said the king. " If
there is anything on earth which will cure
you, my dear, you shall have it, though I
give my kingdom to get it for you! Only
tell me what it is, that I may procure it at
once! "

" It is more than your kingdom," she
replied, with another groan. " It is of such
a nature that I dare not speak of it! " Then
she writhed and shuddered as if in fearful

agony, and the Khan was nigh distracted to see her suffering so.

" Tell me, my love, tell me! " he begged. " No matter what it is, you shall have it! You have my sacred promise! "

" Your son," whispered the wicked woman, "Sunshine has worked an evil charm upon me, and I shall surely die this night if his heart's blood is not given me!"

The Khan shrank from his wife in horror. He loved his eldest child more than life itself, and to kill him would be impossible. Nevertheless, something must be done quickly. " The queen," he thought, " is mad; she must be humored, and there is my kingly word which must not be broken. I will have a goat killed, and its heart given her, and when she is well again, she will be as glad as I that I thus deceived her! " So he drew near the queen and spoke reassuringly to her:

" My love, your life is more precious to me than that of many sons! You shall have the heart's blood of Sunshine this very night without fail. Meanwhile, try to sleep."

He turned toward the door and met Moonshine coming in. One look at the lad's face told him that his last terrible words had been overheard. " I must explain my plan to him," he thought, but at that moment a messenger came to him bearing important news, and he straightway forgot all about the boy.

Moonshine, however, was as one struck dumb with surprise and fear. He had indeed heard part of the conversation between the Khan and his queen, for the two had been talking loudly as he approached their door, and he thought, of course, that his brother was in deadly peril. As soon as he had recovered a little from the shock of his discovery, he ran to find Sunshine and poured the whole story into his ears.

Sunshine was more grieved at the apparent lack of love shown by his father than he was fearful for his own life, but there was no time to weep and lament, for he must leave the palace at once and be far away in some safe hiding-place by nightfall.

"I am going with you!" declared Moonshine.

"Nay," said Sunshine, though he looked grateful. "I know not what dangers and privations I may have to meet. You must not think of it!"

"Indeed, yes!" cried the other. "What will home be without you, dear brother? Your life shall be my life, whatever and wherever it is!"

There was no dissuading him, so in a very short time the two lads had slipped quietly and secretly forth from the palace and were out in the wide world.

All that day they walked, and the next, and the next, sleeping at night wherever they could find shelter. On the third day they came into a barren, desolate country, with no sign of human life to be seen anywhere, and nothing which could yield them water or food. They struggled man-

He found a great red door set deep into the face of
the rock.   *Page* 169.

fully on, but at last Moonshine stumbled
and fell to the earth.

"Alas, dear brother," he said, " I can go
no farther. Bid me farewell and go your
way; there is no need for two of us to die!
As for me, I am so weary that the thought
of death seems pleasant to my mind."

Sunshine did not try to argue with his
brother, but made him as comfortable as
the hot desert sand would allow and bade
him be of good cheer and await his return,
for he would surely find and bring him
help. Then he began looking this way
and that for some sign of a spring or a bit
of an oasis. At last his eye was caught by
a bright red something on the side of a
rocky cliff not far away. He hastened to
see what it might be and found that it was
a great red door set deep into the face of
the rock. His courage rose at the sight,
for a door might have a kindly human
being behind it. He approached and
rapped sturdily upon it, whereupon it was
slowly opened by an old man. Sunshine

was so relieved that he could have fallen upon the stooping shoulders and kissed the long, flowing beard. Quickly he told his story and entreated the old man to give him aid for Moonshine. The hermit, for such he declared himself to be, lost no time in accompanying Sunshine back to where his brother lay, and then he used all his skill to bring the exhausted boy back to health and strength.

At last he was successful, and the long and the short of it all was that the two lads took up their abode with the old hermit and lived with him as his own sons. Indeed, he soon declared that he could have loved no true sons any better. So the weeks and months went on, and the three dwelt happily together in their cave behind the red door in the desert. But as the year drew to a close, a great tragedy befell them.

It happened that the Khan who ruled over this country was a wicked, ill-tempered, suspicious monarch who hated and feared strangers above all men, because of

a prophecy concerning them. It was foretold that he should one day lose his throne
and crown to some lad from a strange
land. And so he had made a law that every
youth who came into his kingdom from another country should be seized at once by
his soldiers and cast into a cave where
lived three fierce demon-bears.

For a long time no one had heard of
the coming of Sunshine and Moonshine,
for very rarely did any stray traveler or
caravan pass the solitary red door in the
cliff. But at length, in some mysterious
way, the Khan learned of the two lads
living with the hermit and sent his soldiers in angry haste to fetch them.

The old man spied the men coming
across the desert and at once guessed their
purpose, so, while they were still far off,
he ran quickly to the two boys and bade
them hide themselves away. Sunshine
climbed into a barrel of mangos, crouch-
ing down until they covered him, and
Moonshine hid in a sack of grain. When

the soldiers reached the red door, the hermit opened it willingly.

" Boys? " said he, in answer to their question. " I have no boys! I am an old man and have lived in this desert place many a long year without wife or child to bear me company. You must be mistaken! "

The soldiers pushed the hermit roughly aside and entered the cave.

" You had better not lie to the Khan's soldiers! " said the captain threateningly.

" I have told you no lie," replied the hermit, " but if you doubt my word, come in, look and see."

For a moment the men hesitated, then, with an oath, the captain seized the hermit by his long white beard and shook him.

" So you thought you would give us the trouble of searching! " said he. " We'll do no such thing! I know there is a boy here, and my orders are to fetch him, so bring him out at once — and I'll teach you to hurry! "

He raised his sword over the hermit's head, but before he could bring it down, Sunshine had leaped from his hiding-place, had caught hold of the captain's arm and had stayed the blow.

" Oho! " said the captain, and he flashed around upon the lad. " So you *are* here, after all — I was almost beginning to doubt! "

There was no use in struggling. The soldiers gathered around Sunshine, bound his hands behind his back, flung him on a horse and, without giving him a moment to bid farewell to the grief-stricken old hermit, rode away with him. Not until they had gone far over the desert on their way to the Khan's city did the captain remember that he had been told there were *two* boys living with the hermit. He stopped abruptly, wheeled his horse and gave orders that the troop should return at once to the old man's cave. Sunshine guessed what was in the captain's mind, and his heart sank within him. " There

will be no possible escape for my brother,"
he thought, " for the soldiers will come
upon Moonshine unexpectedly before he
has time to hide again!" Then he began
planning and wondering if he could not,
by craft, prevent the soldiers from returning. At last he groaned aloud.

" Woe is me!" he said. " Alas! And
woe is me! Would that I had died with
my brother before this evil fate befell me!"

" What do you mean by that?" said the
captain, who had heard his sorrowful
words.

" What should I mean but what I say?"
said Sunshine, with another groan. "When
you stood at the door of our cave we had
but just returned from digging the grave
of my brother. And now, surely, the poor
old man, our foster-father, will die of grief,
for both his sons are lost to him — all in
the space of a day!"

The captain drew rein, and the soldiers
behind him halted respectfully. The heat
of the desert was great, and he had no de-

sire to travel the long distance back to the cave of the red door, to no purpose.

" Young man," he said sternly to Sunshine. " Is it indeed true that your brother is dead, and that there is now no strange youth in the cave of the hermit? "

" Have I not said it? " replied Sunshine impatiently. " Indeed, I know not which I wish the more — that I were dead beside my brother, or that he were here beside me to share my woe! " Then he wept aloud.

The captain hesitated, then he slowly turned his horse and bade his soldiers gruffly to proceed to the palace of the Khan.

Sunshine's heart bounded with joy and relief for his brother, but he still continued to groan and lament, that the soldiers might be deceived.

It was a long distance to the Khan's city, and by the time Sunshine and his cruel captors had reached the gates, the sun was setting. Now it happened that a young and beautiful daughter of the Khan was

at that moment sitting on the low roof of
the palace, enjoying the cool twilight air.
Looking down into the street below, she
saw the line of soldiers riding by, with
Sunshine in their midst, his head bowed
and his hands bound behind him. He
looked up, and his eyes met those of the
princess. The light of the setting sun
rested on his black hair; his face was pale,
and his eyes big and sorrowful. Never,
thought the princess, had she seen so beautiful a youth, and he, looking up at her
as she leaned over the roof, thought she
must be a daughter of the gods, so fair
and lovely she was.

The princess made haste to inquire who
the lad might be and soon learned that he
was a strange youth condemned, because
of the prophecy, to be thrown to the
demon-bears on the morrow. Then she
sought her father, the Khan, and kneeling
before him, she entreated him to spare the
life of this fair young stranger.

Now the Khan lived in daily dread that

the prophecy concerning an unknown young man would come true, so when his daughter urged him to spare this fellow who might be the very one foretold, he fell into a terrible rage. She, not seeing that her cause was hopeless, continued to beg her father for the young man's life. At last the Khan's temper broke all bounds. He summoned his soldiers and, pointing to the princess, cried:

" Take her away! She has more thought for this upstart stranger than for the safety and throne of her father! Take her away, I say, and cast her into a dungeon. And on the morrow choose two strong sacks; tie this strange youth into one of them, my daughter into the other; then cast both into the cave of the demon-bears! "

The princess, though she could have fainted from very terror, was too proud to show her fear, too noble to lament her life, so she silently allowed the rough soldiers to bind her hands and lead her away.

At sunrise the next day everything was prepared as the Khan had ordered, and the two unfortunate young people were thrust into huge sacks which were tied about their necks. Then they were cast into an open, rocky cave by a river, where the demon-bears came daily to drink.

Sunshine sighed deeply as he saw the princess beside him, her fair face and long hair emerging from the mouth of the sack.

" Alas! " said he. " And ten times alas! That I should die is nothing, for what am I but a stranger and an outcast? But oh, the cruel pity of it, that you, loveliest princess, should perish too! "

" Nay, fair youth," said the Khan's daughter, " mourn not for me. I am only an unthinking girl whose life or death can mean nothing to the world — and since it is my father's will that I die thus, willing am I to obey him. But that you, a man of noble birth, unless your looks belie you, should meet such a cruel fate — and only because you are a stranger! Indeed, that seems more than my sad heart can bear! "

While these two noble young creatures were thus lamenting each other's hard lot, forgetful of their own, the three demon-bears drew near and overheard their talk, and the heart of the chief of them was softened at their words. He turned to his companions, saying:

" Of a truth, the unselfishness of these two young mortals moves me to pity! If there is such bravery in the heart of man, I am minded never to eat human flesh again !"

The other two, being also touched by the beauty and nobleness of their captives, readily agreed with the chief; and they resolved to begin at once to be the friends and not the fearful enemies of man. As they entered the cave, they saw that Sunshine and the princess grew white with terror at the sight of them, so the chief called out reassuringly:

" Be not afraid! The heart of a demon-bear is not always as cruel as men say! We

have come, not to devour you but to set
you free. A lad and a lass who, in such a
dire strait, think only of each other, deserve to live long in peace. By my magic
power I declare your bonds broken! Go,
and from henceforth think of the demon-
bears as no longer enemies but friends! "

The wretched sacks dropped from the
sides of Sunshine and the princess, and
they stood up safe and sound and as free
as the wind that blew about them.

The Siddhi-kur ceased speaking, and a
long pause followed, but the Prince said
never a word. Only he stood still a moment and seemed to gurgle unintelligibly
in his throat.

" What did you say? " said the Siddhi-
kur, leaning forward.

Another gurgle, and the Prince turned
his head, whereat the Siddhi-kur burst
into a merry peal of laughter, for wedged
between the lad's teeth was a piece of
wood, making speech impossible.

" You are a wiser youth than I thought,"
said the Siddhi-kur, when he had a little
recovered from his mirth. " Did you put
that wedge in your mouth before I began
my tale, so that you could not speak, no
matter how much you wanted to? "

The Khan's son nodded.

The Siddhi-kur settled back in his sack
with a sigh. "You have won," he said,
" and I might as well resign myself to my
fate! Farewell, dear mango tree and
lovely garden of ghost children! Farewell, for now I must dwell far away in
another cool grove beside the cave of Nagarguna, on the Shining Mountain!

" But I suppose you really deserve to
know the ending of my story," he continued, in a more cheerful tone, " though
you might guess the rest for yourself.

" Of course, the princess went back to
her father, who was nigh dead with repentance now that his wrath had cooled,
and Sunshine hastened to the cave in the
desert to relieve the minds of the good

old hermit and Moonshine, his faithful brother. And then, of course, there was a great royal wedding, a double one — for not only did Sunshine marry the lovely princess, but Moonshine found an almost equally beautiful bride in her younger sister.

" The prophecy which the Khan had dreaded so long came true, but in a very different way than he had expected. He did indeed lose his throne and crown to a strange lad, but he gave them up of his own free will to Sunshine, because he loved the boy so, and because he was old and weary and had no greater wish in life than to see his son and daughter ruling quietly and prosperously over his kingdom. So they all lived happily ever after. And — oh, yes! — they soon paid a visit to Sunshine's father and found him grown old and gray, sorrowing for his two dear sons. The wicked queen had meanwhile died, just because she was too wicked to live. So everybody was happy and satisfied."

A look of great contentment and relief settled upon the face of the Prince, and he moved briskly on again in the direction of the Shining Mountain. At last they saw it gleaming in the distance.

"And now, O Prince," said the Siddhi-kur, "we are nearing the end of our journey. Keep well the lesson of silence you have learned with such pain and labor, for a king who thinks much and speaks little will be a wise monarch, and his people will dwell in peace, happiness and prosperity under his sway."

THE END.